THE
DOUBLE
PORTION
ANOINTING

THE DOUBLE PORTION ANOINTING

ROD PARSLEY

ISBN: 1-880244-73-X
Copyright © 2002 by Rod Parsley.

Published by:
Results Publishing
P.O. Box 32903
Columbus, Ohio 43232-0903, USA

Contents

Your Hour of Power

From the beginning of time there has been a struggle for the double portion of God's blessing destined for the church.

Jacob and Esau struggled for the double portion inheritance.

Perez struggled with his brother to possess his double portion as a firstborn son.

Elisha desired a double portion of Elijah's spirit before he was taken away to heaven. The double portion literally culminated shortly after his death during an Israelite's funeral.

Job's captivity was turned around. When he prayed for his friends, he received twice as much, or a double portion, of all that he previously possessed. He received double for his trouble!

God's promise of a double portion doesn't stop there. The prophet Isaiah said, "Instead of your shame you shall have a double portion, instead of dishonor you shall rejoice in your lot; therefore in your land you shall possess a double portion; yours shall be everlasting joy" (61:7 RSV).

Since the resurrection of Jesus Christ, the church has been in a fight to receive the double portion inheritance that rightfully belongs to her. But I believe we are at a prophetic crossroads, if you will, in history.

We have entered the third millennium, or the third day, since Jesus traversed the earth seeking to save those who were lost—a people with a birthright—those destined to walk in a double portion of His Spirit, just as Elisha received a double portion of Elijah's spirit.

As part of the church of the firstborn, God has saved us, the best, for last. I am reminded of Jesus' first miracle, recorded in the Gospel of John, with His call to ministry commencing at a wedding in Cana:

> *And the third day there was a marriage in Cana of Galilee; and the mother of Jesus was there: And both Jesus was called, and his disciples, to the marriage.*
>
> *And when they wanted wine, the mother of Jesus saith unto him, They have no wine. Jesus saith unto her, Woman, what have I to do with thee? mine hour is not yet come.*
>
> *His mother saith unto the servants, Whatsoever he saith unto you, do it.*
>
> *And there were set there six waterpots of stone, after the manner of the purifying of the Jews, containing two or three firkins apiece.*
>
> *Jesus saith unto them, Fill the waterpots with water. And they filled them up to the brim. And he saith unto them, Draw out now, and bear unto the governor of the feast. And they bare it.*

> *When the ruler of the feast had tasted the water that was made wine, and knew not whence it was: (but the servants which drew the water knew;) the governor of the feast called the bridegroom, and saith unto him, Every man at the beginning doth set forth good wine; and when men have well drunk, then that which is worse: but thou hast kept the good wine until now.*

> *This beginning of miracles did Jesus in Cana of Galilee, and manifested forth his glory; and his disciples believed on him (John 2:1-11).*

Jesus' very first miracle was not reserved to wipe the blindness out of Bartimaeus' eyes. He was not destined to first stop the woman's issue of blood. The first encounter with the supernatural was not Jesus' command to Peter to get out of the boat, step on the troubled sea, and walk to Him.

The first display of Jesus Christ, the Anointed One and His anointing, was not to demand that Lazarus, wrapped in grave clothes, come forth out of the tomb.

All of these were great displays of God's power and anointing, and are recorded forever within the pages of His Holy Word. Yet, these miracles were merely in response to needs.

The very first miracle Jesus reserved to show us the character of our Father, and to announce unequivocally that God is not just interested in meeting your need. He is a God of more than enough, too much, overflow, and double for your trouble. And, He has saved His church, the best, for last to display His tangible anointing and power to a sin-sick, disease-ridden, and burden-stricken world.

The double portion is not only a desire, it is a right of every born-again believer. God wants to give you your double portion more than you want to receive it. He wants to give you more than enough healing, victory, joy, and anointing!

The Lord Almighty is about to catapult you out of the ordinary and into the extraordinary, out of the natural and into the supernatural. When you experience the Holy Spirit's anointing, you will never be the same again.

Therefore, we must refuse to settle for the mundane and the mediocre. We must bring every thought captive from being anything less than Holy Ghost possessed. We must desire nothing less than the anointing that destroys yokes of bondage, opens blind eyes, straightens crippled limbs, mends broken homes and delivers every captive!

My heart's cry is, "Get ready!" There is a storm of revival coming! There is a double portion of Holy Ghost wine, oil, and anointing waiting for you. The Book of Joel proclaims it this way, "Be glad then, ye children of Zion, and rejoice in the Lord your God: for he hath given you the former rain moderately, and he will cause to come down for you the rain, the former rain, and the latter rain in the first month. And the floors shall be full of wheat, and the fats shall overflow with wine and oil" (2:23,24).

God's Word promises that there will be an overflow, or a double portion, of wine and oil, or anointing, coming together in one month. That's a double blessing!

This book will reveal to you the double portion anointing that is waiting for you. It is a part of your inheritance through Jesus Christ. It will show you how to walk in the anointing of the Holy Spirit and do greater works than that of our risen Messiah.

The Lord is giving birth, in this third day of prophetic destiny, to a brand of people who will learn to live, move, and have their being in the spirit realm because of the anointing upon their lives. Will you answer the call to be a part of this remnant, destined to walk in the double portion of God's Spirit?

This is your hour of power. This is your day to receive your double portion.

Chapter One

A Dead Man's Double Portion

Have you ever noticed the parallel between the book of Acts and the book of Second Kings? The stories have similar beginnings. One prophet is to be caught up while His disciples look on. The other prophet is to be taken away in a chariot of fire.

One leader, Jesus Christ, leaves His followers the promise, "that they shall receive power, after that the Holy Ghost is come upon you" (Acts 1:8). What kind of power? It is greater power. For Jesus said, "Greater works than these shall he do; because I go unto my Father" (John 14:12). The other, Elijah, promised his follower, Elisha, "If you see me when I go, you shall receive a double portion." (See 2 Kings 2:9-11.)

Elisha received the double portion, performing twice as many miracles as Elijah, but it took his own death to fulfill this word.

A DEAD MAN RAISED TO LIFE

When Elisha became ill near to death, King Joash visited him and wept, exclaiming, "My father, my father, the chariot of Israel, and horsemen thereof." This was the same thing Elisha had done before Elijah was taken up to heaven. (See 2 Kings 3:14 and 2:12.)

Elisha then died in his bed like anyone else. Josephus, the Jewish historian, recorded that he had a grand funeral. Joash and the people paid great tribute to the prophet who had served Israel for more than fifty years. Along with Elijah, he was one of the greatest influences for righteousness and a prophetic voice of protection in some of the most difficult times facing the nation.

The Bible records, "And Elisha died, and they buried him. And the bands of the Moabites invaded the land at the coming in of the year" (2 Kings 13:20).

It is important to note that the graves of the Jews were not like ours, but were instead caves cut in the side of a rock. The opening was sealed by a heavy, huge stone. The body of Elisha was not put into a coffin either, but was wrapped in grave clothes.

Within a year of Elisha's death, Israel was threatened by a band of Moabites. Today, it would be similar to a border attack upon a nation. They destroyed their crops and flocks. It was during such a raid that a magnificent miracle occurred.

Second Kings shows what happened next. "And it came to pass, as they were burying a man, that, behold, they spied a band of men; and they cast the man into the sepulchre of Elisha: and when the man was let down, and touched the bones of Elisha, he revived, and stood up on his feet" (vs. 21).

The Israelites had a comrade in arms that was struck down in battle and then died. Now they had his body with them when suddenly their enemies came and ambushed them. I can only imagine the commotion as they said amongst themselves, "We don't have time to bury this man, or we will end up just like him—dead."

For the purpose of escaping from the enemy, the Israelites threw this man into the tomb of Elisha. In their haste, they may have been unaware that it was this great prophet's tomb or that there were even old, dry, dead bones in there.

In a matter of moments, the race was on! While the Israelites were fleeing their enemy, they looked over their shoulder and saw the dead man they threw in that pit running behind them. For when the dead man touched Elisha's bones, he came to life again, and rose up on his feet. There was still enough of the tangible anointing of God residing upon the prophet Elisha's dead body to raise a man from the dead. If that much anointing is in a dead man's bones, how much is inside you?

THE DOUBLE PORTION

This miracle was Elisha's greatest. It showed the tangibility of the anointing long after the prophet had died. The effect of this supernatural resurrection stirred the soul of the nation of Israel, during a turbulent time of war, to have confidence that God was with them.

However, I believe there is something more significant about this miracle. In order to understand its importance we must go back in time to when a great transference of anointing was passed from Elisha's predecessor, Elijah, to him. Second Kings 2:9-12 records:

> *And it came to pass, when they were gone over, that Elijah said unto Elisha, Ask what I shall do for thee, before I be taken away from thee. And Elisha said, I pray thee, let a double portion of thy spirit be upon me.*

And he said, Thou hast asked a hard thing: nevertheless, if thou see me when I am taken from thee, it shall be so unto thee; but if not, it shall not be so.

And it came to pass, as they still went on, and talked, that, behold, there appeared a chariot of fire, and horses of fire, and parted them both asunder; and Elijah went up by a whirlwind into heaven.

And Elisha saw it, and he cried, My father, my father, the chariot of Israel, and the horsemen thereof. And he saw him no more: and he took hold of his own clothes, and rent them in two pieces.

According to the law, Elisha made his request to receive a double portion—the same as the firstborn received of his father's inheritance. (See Deuteronomy 21:17.) Elisha thought of himself as Elijah's firstborn son more than did the other "sons of the prophets." Elijah, himself, had already anointed him to be his successor and carry on the work of the ministry. (See 1 Kings 19:16.)

Both custom and common sense suggest that Elisha did not desire a double measure of Elijah's spirit. It is impossible for a man to leave to his heir more than he possesses. The double portion mentioned here refers to the fact that Elisha performed a greater number of miracles than Elijah, a proof that the spirit of Elijah rested doubly upon him.

Elijah's response, that he "asked a hard thing" in

relation to the double portion, only served to prove that the request was not his to fulfill but God's alone. In order to receive "the double portion," Elisha had to witness Elijah's departure from the earth.

When the chariots of heaven came for Elijah, he was not found praying, but instead was edifying, instructing, and encouraging his son in the faith, Elisha. He was concerned with the kingdom of God.

The same held true when Jesus was taken to heaven after His resurrection. He was not praying or waiting but was working with His disciples. He was giving them their marching orders to fulfill His plan upon the earth. The book of Acts states of Jesus:

> *To whom also he shewed himself alive after his passion by many infallible proofs, being seen of them forty days, and speaking of the things pertaining to the kingdom of God: and, being assembled together with them, commanded them that they should not depart from Jerusalem, but wait for the promise of the Father, which, saith he, ye have heard of me. For John truly baptized with water; but ye shall be baptized with the Holy Ghost not many days hence.*

> *But ye shall receive power, after that the Holy Ghost is come upon you: and ye shall be witnesses unto me both in Jerusalem, and in all Judaea, and in Samaria, and unto the uttermost part of the earth. And when he had spoken these things, while they beheld, he was taken up; and a cloud received him out of their sight (1:3, 8, 9).*

Preparation for heaven is not merely found in prayer but in working in the harvest fields—so that we are not found sleeping when Jesus appears. I'm reminded of the story of a dear friend who was asking God for the anointing.

One day, she decided to lock herself in the bathroom and pray until she received the anointing of the Holy Spirit upon her life. She grabbed hold of the toilet and began fervently praying and weeping for the anointing. She said, "God, give me the anointing! God, I can't live without the anointing!" All of a sudden the Spirit of the Lord interrupted her, called her name and said on the inside of her, "The toilet isn't sick."

The point of this story is that the anointing is not just for us to enjoy. It is given to every believer to meet the needs of those around them.

When the double portion of Elijah's spirit was passed on to Elisha, it was to carry on the work that Elijah had already begun. But if Elisha received the double portion as a firstborn son, how can you and I claim a double portion of the anointing?

THE CHURCH OF THE FIRSTBORN

The book of Hebrews proclaims, "But ye are come unto mount Sion, and unto the city of the living God, the heavenly Jerusalem, and to an innumerable company of angels, to the general assembly and church of the first-born, which are written in heaven, and to God the Judge of all, and to the spirits of just men made perfect" (12:22,23).

The word, "firstborn" in these verses brings to mind many significant meanings. For example, the word "first" means foremost in time, place, or order of importance. The word "born" denotes the hour when something already in existence is manifested.

Jesus Christ is the Alpha and Omega, the beginning and the end. But there came a time when He was revealed to be the "first begotten in the world." (See Hebrews 1:6.) He is also the firstborn son, the firstborn of creation, the firstborn from the dead, and the firstborn among many brethren. (See Luke 2:7, Colossians 1:15, Colossians 1:8, and Romans 8:29.)

Historically, the firstborn of Israel had their names written upon a scroll. Similarly, all believers, as firstborn heirs with Christ, have their names written in heaven and are enrolled as citizens there. Therefore, saints of God are considered "firstborn" in God's kingdom through adoption into the body of Christ.

Just as Elisha enjoyed special privileges, namely a double portion of Elijah's spirit, so you and I can receive a double portion of the anointing as joint-heirs with Jesus. In other words, by becoming a born-again believer, we have become identified with Jesus and can partake of all of the rights bestowed upon a firstborn son. The double portion that is bestowed upon every believer is the same one described in 1 John, "But ye have an unction from the Holy One, and ye know all things" (2:20).

THE TANGIBLE ANOINTING

The ministries of Elijah and Elisha are filled with displays of the tangible anointing of God.

Elijah raised a mother's son to life by laying upon his dead body. Elisha did the same with a Shunammite woman's son—her only child. (See 2 Kings 4.)

As I described earlier, it was the tangible anointing that was transferred to the dead Israelite when he was raised to life after coming in contact with Elisha's dead bones.

Throughout the Bible, the tangible anointing was present. It was found in Moses' rod that parted the Red Sea and brought water from a rock. (See Exodus 14:15,16,21 and 17:4-6.) It could be seen in Peter's shadow and Paul's handkerchiefs and aprons. (See Acts 5:14,15 and 19:11,12.)

The prophet Isaiah, described the anointing in this way: "And it shall come to pass in that day, that his burden shall be taken away from off thy shoulder, and his yoke from off thy neck, and the yoke shall be destroyed because of the anointing" (vs. 10:27).

The yoke on the neck of an oxen was an actual collar. Because of the pressure of the fat of the oxen's strong neck against the collar, or yoke, it could snap and be destroyed.

In this passage of Scripture, the word yoke represents oppression. The word oppression commonly means to rule over or have authority over someone. The tangible anointing working to destroy the yoke of infirmity can be vividly seen in Jesus' ministry. The Gospel of Luke documents, "And, behold, there was a woman which had a spirit of infirmity eighteen years, and was bowed together, and could in no wise lift up herself.

"And when Jesus saw her, he called her to him, and said unto her, Woman, thou art loosed from thine infirmity. And he laid his hands on her: and immediately she was made straight, and glorified God" (13:11-13).

This woman had a spirit of infirmity or oppression. This spirit was lord over her body, causing her to be bent over. But the tangible anointing came when Jesus laid His hands upon her to deliver her from this yoke of bondage.

That same tangible anointing is available to you today. It is time for anything other than Jesus—be it infirmity, sickness, addiction, disease, or alcoholism which is trying to lord over you—to recognize who is the Lord of your life.

In today's society, people from every socioeconomic, geographical, and ethnic background have a yoke of oppression ruling over them. For some, their bodies lord over them. Some people are ruled by their thoughts and vain imaginations. Others are addicted to drugs, alcohol, or television. Many are driven into despair and depression and are on the verge of suicide. Why? Because the yoke of oppression has formed a stronghold about their necks.

When something other than God has pre-eminence in your life, then it has become an idol to you. An idol is anything to which lordship is directed in your life. First John 5:21 declares, "Little children, keep yourselves from idols." He wasn't necessarily talking about you setting up a Buddha in your living room.

Lordship is anything that has authority over you. If there's anything right now that has authority over you, it is my prayer that, before you finish this book, a river of living water will swell up on the inside of you and that yoke of oppression will be destroyed because of the anointing.

SIGNS AND WONDERS FOR OUR GENERATION

Just as the double portion displayed in Elisha's body to raise a dead man became a sign for Israel's victory over the Moabites, so God wants to use you and me to become signs and wonders to a lost and dying world. The Bible says, "Behold, I and the children whom the Lord hath given me are for signs and for wonders in Israel from the Lord of hosts, which dwelleth in mount Zion" (Isaiah 8:18).

What are signs and wonders? A sign is an instrument that points individuals to something beyond itself. In the past when I've shared this revelation at my church, I tell those visiting us that I'm glad that when they got there, they didn't stand around the sign that says, "World Harvest Church" and say, "Well, I'm glad I came to World Harvest Church today." No, the sign is just something used to direct people here.

People are supposed to be able to look at you and me and find their way to Jesus. We are supposed to be signs and wonders. A wonder can be defined as the display of the mighty acts of God that only He could accomplish. This ministry is a sign and a wonder.

Nearly a quarter of a century ago when I first began in ministry, I wrote down in the back of my old Bible, "Lord, do things so incredible that men would have to look beyond humanity and look to God and say no man could have done this." That's a wonder.

Signs and wonders are given to confirm to broken and dejected people that there is still a God who is able to save, heal, and deliver them, regardless of any circumstances they may be facing. They originate with the body of Christ. People in the world are looking for something greater than themselves. If we do not display God's power and anointing, then the devil will gladly oblige them with lying signs and wonders.

In Mark chapter 16, Jesus gave the Church this Great Commission:

Go ye into all the world, and preach the gospel to every creature. He that believeth and is baptized shall be saved; but he that believeth not shall be damned.

And these signs shall follow them that believe; In my name shall they cast out devils; they shall speak with new tongues; they shall take up serpents; and if they drink any deadly thing, it shall not hurt them; they shall lay hands on the sick, and they shall recover (vv. 15-18).

What is the first sign that will follow us? We will cast out devils. I like to say it this way. We will take on the devil! We are not waiting for him to attack us, our family, or our neighbors, but we are proceeding into enemy-held territory to take back what rightfully belongs to us. We are not on the defensive, running like scared animals with our tails tucked between our legs. No, we are on the offensive!

Second, these verses say if we drink any deadly thing it shall not harm us. There is a protective covering over us because of the anointing of God upon our lives. However, it doesn't stop there. The next thing we are to do is to lay hands on the sick and watch them recover.

The next verse is where we begin to see Jesus' involvement and His anointing at work within us to meet the needs of people in this end-time hour. "So then after the Lord had spoken unto them, he was received up into heaven, and sat on the right hand of God. And they went forth, and preached every where, the Lord working with them, and confirming the word with signs following. Amen" (Mark 16:19,20).

Jesus worked with the disciples! They did not go out alone on an impossible mission. They took the anointing— a double portion, as part of the church of the firstborn— with them!

I like to explain the meaning of the word "work" in verse 20 as motion against resistance. There is supposed to be resistance when you're working. For example, running a vacuum cleaner is work because it doesn't just run itself. You have to put some energy behind it. In the same manner, Jesus worked.

Do you have any resistance in your life? If so, then I have good news for you. God will give you motion against that resistance. It is called the anointing. It swells up out of your belly in times of adversity and propels you through every line of Satan's defense. The Lord gives you motion not only against the resistance, but to break you through the barrier keeping you from your blessing.

Not only did Jesus work with the disciples, He also "confirmined" His word. Webster's says to confirm means to remove all doubt by performing indisputable acts of authority.[1]

I think it's time for the skeptics, scorners, naysayers, and doubters to be silenced. But the only way to stop the onslaught of slander against Jesus Christ, the Anointed One and His anointing, is to display signs and wonders on the earth.

A lukewarm church cannot compete with the devil's lying signs and wonders because they are not allowing Jesus to "confirm" His word. They are busy doing their own thing—marketing their meetings, plotting their plans and placing their priorities above God's.

The only way to stop the onslaught of slander against Jesus Christ, the Anointed One and His anointing, is to display His power on the earth. People with no hope and skeptics who are driven by doubt need to witness a Messiah who is a wonder and a wonder-worker! They need to witness, through us, that He is indeed risen just as He said, and His anointing is working on the inside of us to show them our risen Savior!

LIVING IN THE SUPERNATURAL REALM

How tragic to go through your daily routine only to make it to heaven and hear the Lord say, "But I had so much more to give to you if only you would have asked me." Many people do. But there are a few, a remnant, who have made the decision to have all of Jesus and His anointing that they can.

The prophet Elisha was one of those people. He stood head and shoulders above the other prophets because he not only knew the law and the promise of the double portion but he dared to ask for and operate in it.

When you get to the point that you want the anointing more than you want your next breath, it will begin to manifest in your life. The Bible promises, "And this is the confidence that we have in him, that, if we ask any thing according to his will, he heareth us: and if we know that he hear us, whatsoever we ask, we know that we have the petitions that we desired of him" (1 John 5:14,15).

The Lord will touch you and you will be changed. When you realize you can have this same double portion, you will never be the same again. You will refuse the mundane and the mediocre. You will walk on the earth as a spirit man led and anointed by the Spirit of God. And, there will be proof, signs and wonders, to attest to the anointing of the Holy Spirit upon your life.

As a part of the church of the firstborn, there is a double portion waiting for you and me. All we must do is receive it. Make no mistake—there will be mountains to traverse and valleys to cross, but there is a double portion of the anointing residing on the inside of us to take us all the way to victory!

Chapter Two

Mountain-Moving Faith

An inheritance is only valuable if you receive it and use it. The same holds true with the double portion you, as a child of God, are promised. If you do not appropriate the power given to you through the Holy Spirit, then you will continue living life as you always have.

Faith is a key element. The subject of faith is one of my favorites. Why? Faith in God can move a mighty mountain. Faith in God can cool the fevered brow of an infant child. Faith in God can make the desert seem like a garden. Faith in God can put bread on the table when there is nothing in the cupboard. Faith in God can bring you the victory and help you operate in the double portion He has for you!

THE WALLS CAME DOWN BY FAITH

Under the command of Joshua the Israelites were people of faith. They didn't just possess a halfhearted faith. They possessed "wall crumbling" faith.

The Book of Joshua gives an explicit look at Israel's first and greatest battle in their new homeland, the battle of Jericho, and the great faith it would take to defeat their enemy.

Now Jericho was straitly shut up because of the children of Israel: none went out, and none came in. And the Lord said unto Joshua, See, I have given into thine hand Jericho, and the king thereof, and the mighty men of valour.

And ye shall compass the city, all ye men of war, and go round about the city once. Thus shalt thou do six days. And seven priests shall bear before the ark seven trumpets of rams' horns: and the seventh day ye shall compass the city seven times, and the priests shall blow with the trumpets.

And it shall come to pass, that when they make a long blast with the ram's horn, and when ye hear the sound of the trumpet, all the people shall shout with a great shout; and the wall of the city shall fall down flat, and the people shall ascend up every man straight before him.

And Joshua had commanded the people, saying, Ye shall not shout, nor make any noise with your voice, neither shall any word proceed out of your mouth, until the day I bid you shout; then shall ye shout.

And it came to pass at the seventh time, when the priests blew with the trumpets, Joshua said unto the people, Shout; for the Lord hath given you the city.

> *So the people shouted when the priests*
> *blew with the trumpets: and it came to pass,*
> *when the people heard the sound of the trumpet,*
> *and the people shouted with a great shout, that*
> *the wall fell down flat, so that the people went*
> *up into the city, every man straight before him,*
> *and they took the city (6:1-5, 10, 16, 20).*

It is important to note that verse one says the city of Jericho was shut up because of the children of Israel. The fact of the matter was the heathen people of Jericho were more afraid of the Israelites than the Israelites were of them. The source of your fear is actually fearful of you as well. Whatever tries to strike fear and terror in your heart is, in reality, more fearful of you than you are of it!

The devil knows what sometimes you forget. That is, "Greater is he that is in you, than he that is in the world" (1 John 4:4). If God be for you, who can be against you? (See Romans 8:31.) No weapon formed against you shall prosper, and every tongue that rises against you in judgment you shall condemn. (See Isaiah 54:17.) A thousand shall fall at your side, and ten thousand at your right side, but it shall not come nigh you. (See Psalm 91:7.)

The cancer that you are afraid of is afraid of you. The financial situation that's looming darkly over your countenance is more fearful of you than you are of it. You have a double portion, and God has given you dominion, power, authority, and anointing!

As I was studying this passage of Scripture, God said to me, "The Israelites were facing what they perceived to be a hopeless situation. All they had was a word: 'I have given into thine hand Jericho.'"

Defeating this well-fortified city had nothing to do with Israel but instead with simplistic obedience to the command of God. If they would obey, He would give them the victory.

THE HALL OF FAITH

The children of Israel knew what it meant to trust in the word of the Lord to bring to pass their miracle. The Hall of Faith records, "By faith the walls of Jericho fell down, after they were compassed about seven days" (Hebrews 11:30).

Did you notice this verse did not say, "By marching the walls fell down"? Neither did it say, "By shouting the walls fell down." The shout was simply the mechanism upon which the delivering power of faith rode. Wishing for something never made it become a reality.

It was not the children of Israel who brought the walls of Jericho down. It was faith in the Lord and taking Him at His word. Faith in God became the catalyst upon which their obedience would ride and the faith of God would be expressed.

The just shall live by faith. (See Romans 1:17.) Regardless of what other religious activity you are involved in, without faith it is impossible to please God. (See Hebrews 11:6.) But with faith all things are possible to Him that believeth. (See Mark 9:23.)

You may be facing a hopeless situation today. You may feel like your family will never be saved. You may be cast down, cast off, cast aside, pushed down, pushed back, and pushed aside. People may say, "Your business will never make it. You will go be bankrupt." The doctors may have told you that you have a disease that is inoperable and incurable. But faith says—regardless of the trouble, tragedy, or trial you or your family may be facing—it will be turned into a testimony of triumph. God will give you His faith-filled Word to rest upon!

FAITH IS NOW

In this end-time hour, we need "right now" faith. Faith is now! The Book of Hebrews records these words:

> *Now faith is the substance of things hoped for, the evidence of things not seen. For by it the elders obtained a good report. Through faith we understand that the worlds were framed by the word of God, so that things which are seen were not made of things which do appear (11:1-3).*

The Bible does not say that faith is the substance of everything. The Bible says that faith is the substance of a very specific group of things. Faith is the substance of things you hope for. So if there is no hope, there can be no faith.

Faith is also the substance, or the tangibility, of everything you hope for. It is the evidence of things not seen. Evidence takes the place of something until whatever you are believing for shows up. For instance, defense lawyers present evidence before a jury in order to persuade them of their client's innocence. The more evidence they can present, the greater likelihood they will be believed and, thus, win their case.

Galatians 3:13 proclaims, "Christ hath redeemed us from the curse of the law, being made a curse for us: for it is written, Cursed is every one that hangeth on a tree." I believe the word "redeemed" signifies a return to the original state of affairs. We have been returned to that point in Genesis which states,

> *And God said, Let us make man in our image, after our likeness: and let them have dominion over the fish of the sea, and over the fowl of the air, and over the cattle, and over all the earth, and over every creeping thing that creepeth upon the earth. So God created man in his own image, in the image of God created he him; male and female created he them (1:26,27).*

We were made in the image of God. He put His character in us which will produce His characteristics through us! We have a spirit in us which is the breath of the Almighty! (See Job 32:8.)

By faith, we understand that the worlds were framed. If we have been redeemed, then what the devil did in the first Adam was not nearly as great as what God did in the second Adam, Jesus Christ. So, in fact, we have a better covenant based upon better promises.

But the Book of Hebrews shows the faith of old covenant believers was nothing to take for granted. For by faith, under the old covenant, men stopped the violence of the sword. Others quenched fires and women received their dead children raised to life again.

Through the blood of Jesus Christ, however, you and I have stepped into a new covenant, based on better promises. This covenant was not ratified by the blood of sheep, goats, and turtle doves, but by the Lamb of God, who was without spot or blemish, slain from the foundation of the world.

The reality is that most Christians are operating way beneath their privileges, or the double portion, God has for them.

It doesn't take much to believe God for your miracle. All it takes is faith no bigger than a grain of mustard seed, and God's Word shows you how you obtain it. (See Matthew 17:20.)

FAITH COMES THREE WAYS

Faith is not confusing. Faith is the substance of things hoped for, the evidence of things not seen. Mountain-moving faith can come three ways.

First, faith comes by hearing. Romans 10:17 says, "So then faith cometh by hearing, and hearing by the word of God." It takes a preacher to bring the Word of God to people lost in their sins. For the Book of Romans also declares, "How then shall they call on him in whom they have not believed? and how shall they believe in him of whom they have not heard? and how shall they hear without a preacher?" (vs. 14). Once we hear that Word, we have the opportunity to receive or reject it.

The *second* way faith comes is through the measure of faith that every person is dealt. The Bible says it this way, "For I say, through the grace given unto me, to every man that is among you, not to think of himself more highly than he ought to think; but to think soberly, according as God hath dealt to every man the measure of faith" (Romans 12:3).

The *third* way you receive faith is through impartation. Timothy received an impartation of faith from Paul when Paul laid his hands upon him. Second Timothy records, "When I call to remembrance the unfeigned faith that is in thee, which dwelt first in thy grandmother Lois, and thy mother Eunice; and I am persuaded that in thee also. Wherefore I put thee in remembrance that thou stir up the gift of God, which is in thee by the putting on of my hands" (1:5,6).

It is not hard to have faith when you understand what faith is. God never demands faith in Him beyond your experience with Him. When you have an experience of faith with God, it's not difficult to trust Him. Why? Because faith comes by hearing, and that produces information which gives you knowledge that, in turn, gives you understanding. Understanding then produces trust, and trust is faith.

We need the God kind of faith. What kind of faith is that? It is faith that calls those things that be not as though they were. (See Romans 4:17.) But there is an obstacle which the devil tries to put in the way of your faith. That obstacle is tradition.

TRADITION: THE THIEF OF POWER

Tradition is the thief of power. It is the thief of faith and hope! First Peter 1:18,19 declare, "Forasmuch as ye know that ye were not redeemed with corruptible things, as silver and gold, from your vain conversation received by tradition from your fathers; but with the precious blood of Christ, as of a lamb without blemish and without spot."

Colossians 2:8 says it another way, "Beware lest any man spoil you through philosophy and vain deceit, after the tradition of men, after the rudiments of the world, and not after Christ."

Tradition will steal your faith in three ways. *First*, it takes doubt to school, and produces unbelief. God can still move even when there is doubt, because doubt questions the existence of something. Doubt says, "I wonder if it could be." However, unbelief declares, "I know it cannot be." Tradition will school you in the art of producing unbelief.

Second, tradition makes the Word of God of no effect because it trains you to do two things. First, it conditions you to ignore the power of Satan, or to trivialize the Anti-Christ spirit. Tradition wants you to dress the devil up in a red suit with horns and a forked tail. It also tries to get you to refuse to acknowledge the existence of a literal God and devil. It will cause you to look at demon power, which is specifically forbidden in the Word of God, as inconsequential.

Even the Bible proclaims that the great archangel, Michael "when contending with the devil he disputed about the body of Moses, durst not bring against him a railing accusation, but said, The Lord rebuke thee" (Jude 9).

Second, tradition not only causes you to disregard satanic power, but it also trains you to be ignorant of your own power. It will train you in the art of being a weak-kneed, patty-cake Christian.

I have witnessed tradition's work in the lives of people during my many years of ministry. One particular story stands out in my mind.

Several years ago, a young girl and her parents came to our church. She had a deadly disease for which there was no cure. When they brought her to one of our services, she was literally at death's door.

While the Word of God was being preached the anointing went into her body. She rose off her bed of affliction, and for several years lived in divine health with a completely clean bill of health from her physicians.

Months later, we decided we weren't going to sing as much out of the hymnals as we did at one time. Instead, we were going to put words up on the screen and sing choruses of praise and worship unto God. Her parents became so incensed at this break with tradition that they left the church and took her with them.

About a year and-a-half later, I received a phone call. It was the parents of that young girl. They asked me, "Could you please come to our home? Our daughter is dying."

I drove to their house, and the moment I got out of my automobile, I sensed in my spirit the spirit of death. When I entered their home there was such a stench penetrating the air that it almost took away my breath. I could hear that young girl gasping for breath in her bedroom.

As I followed the horrible sounds exuding from her room, I became incensed. When I entered the bedroom, it looked more like a funeral parlor than a teenager's hangout. The lights were dim, candles lit the room and soft music played in the background.

On the bed laid the young girl I had come to know, once a picture of health who had been miraculously healed. Now she was nothing more than skin and bones, and fighting just to stay alive.

At the foot of the bed knelt the family's new pastor and his wife. As I walked in, they saw me and motioned for me to kneel in prayer beside them.

I said to this pastor, "Excuse me, what are you doing?" In the faintest whisper they said, "We're praying."

I said, "Well, are you afraid someone will hear you?"

I moved around them, climbed up on the middle of the bed, grabbed that young girl and said, "In the name of Jesus Christ of Nazareth, I rebuke you! You spirit of death, come out of her!"

Less than a week later she was in our Sunday morning service again. She began to regain her weight, and she looked like the specimen of health.

Not long after that, this family left our church again because of some other tradition. Three months later, I attended that young girl's funeral. Because of her parents' desire to "keep with tradition" it seems their daughter paid with her life. Tradition will kill you with a hangnail if you let it.

The *third* way tradition steals your faith and hope is through training you to refuse to call those things that be not as though they are. It will keep you from offering "the sacrifice of praise to God continually, that is, the fruit of our lips giving thanks to his name" (Hebrews 13:15).

Tradition will not allow you to bear fruit in the middle of the winter of your life. It will only keep you holding onto a meager existence of just getting by while it robs you of your anointing and of your double portion.

SPEAKING YOUR WORLD INTO EXISTENCE

Like the children of Israel, this is the year we conquer our Jericho and possess our promised land. What is your Jericho? It is anything keeping you from receiving the double portion God has for you! Colossians 3:16 exhorts us to "let the word of Christ dwell in you richly in all wisdom; teaching and admonishing one another in psalms and hymns and spiritual songs, singing with grace in your hearts to the Lord."

Once you defeat tradition in your life, you then must begin to speak God's Word in faith about your situation. You have the anointing! You have the power. Now, you must put actions with your ability! James 2:26 declares, "For as the body without the spirit is dead, so faith without works is dead also."

You create your world by declaring the Word of God into your future! Begin now to speak to the walls that have kept you from your double portion!

In the darkness of your despair, when everybody says you should cave in and give up, allow faith to arise on the inside of you and proclaim, "I will live even when the doctors have already signed my death certificate!"

Make this declaration of faith: "I shall live and not die. I am healed, and I am whole. I am strong and not weak. The life of God abides in me forever! I am blessed coming in, and I am blessing going out. I declare a thing and God establishes it."

Each morning, begin to announce to the principalities and powers of the air what your day shall hold. Declare salvation over your family. Proclaim that the Holy Spirit will baptize every person in your family. Speak to your bank account and command it to prosper. Begin to speak to your car and command it to drive longer than anybody else's car. Announce to yourself that you determine to be holy, pure, and righteous. You increase in wisdom and favor with God and with men.

Begin to declare what your destiny will be. Then the next time someone asks you, "How are you today?" . . . respond to them, "I don't know. I don't ask myself how I am. According to the Word of the living God, I'm healthy, wealthy, and wise!"

I believe even now you are being filled with faith. Most people don't have a future, they only have a prolonged today—because they have no hope. But I believe you have hope to take the limits off of God and receive the double portion He has for you!

Chapter Three

Will You Be Made Whole?

In this present hour, it is unnerving when you recognize that our society has relegated healing to mind over matter and masqueraded counseling as deliverance. Therefore, there is no yearning for the miraculous because people are ignorant of God's Word and His desire to meet their needs. The result is not only a "just getting by" mentality but also a missed opportunity to receive the double portion the Lord has for them.

It was in a similar setting that Jesus found Himself when He walked in the midst of a sin-infected, unbelieving world. The Bible attests, "And he could there do no mighty work, save that he laid his hands upon a few sick folk, and healed them. And he marvelled because of their unbelief. And he went round about the villages, teaching" (Mark 6:5,6).

You see, healing to God is not even a mighty work. In fact, it is natural. It is so basic that Jesus said healing is the children's bread. (See Mark 7:27.)

Mark, chapter 6, says Jesus marveled because of their unbelief. Notice that it did not say Jesus marveled at their doubt, because doubt does not destroy the miracle-working power of God. Rather, unbelief stops the flow of God's anointing.

Therefore, Jesus began traveling throughout their villages and teaching the people the Word of God. Teaching counters the actions of unbelief. When you get unbelief out of the way, you realize that healing is elementary. When unbelief comes in, the only way to destroy it is by teaching. This is the reason He sent His Word—so that you may be healed. (See Psalm 107:20.)

That is why this chapter is so important to receiving your double portion. In the next few pages, I want to show you the three questions which must be asked and answered in order for you to receive your healing. One is, "Will Jesus heal you?" Two is, "Can Jesus heal you?" Three is, "Will you be made whole?"

As you read on, keep in mind that these questions are not merely just for healing but for whatever you need from the Lord—whether it is deliverance, joy, hope, a marriage restored, salvation for a family member, or a financial breakthrough.

WILL JESUS HEAL YOU?

The first question that must be answered as you approach the Lord to receive your healing is this: Is it Jesus' will to heal me? A leper asked Jesus this in the Gospel of Mark:

> *And there came a leper to him, beseeching him, and kneeling down to him, and saying unto him, If thou wilt, thou canst make me clean. And Jesus, moved with compassion, put forth his hand, and touched him, and saith unto him, I will; be thou clean. And as soon as he had spoken, immediately the leprosy departed from him, and he was cleansed (1:40-42).*

The leper needed assurance from Jesus that it was His will to heal him. Where there is doubt concerning the perfect will of God to give you your miracle, faith can never exist. As I shared in the last chapter, although someone can pray with you to receive your miracle, and you receive it—you must learn how to operate in faith for yourself in order to keep it.

Several years ago I used to get on my knees and pray, "Oh, God! If it be thy will . . ." about whatever situation I was facing in my own life. That was before I began to study God's Word for myself and discovered that beyond a shadow of a doubt it is His will to save, heal, and deliver.

Do you know what I received for praying "Oh, God! If it be thy will . . ."? I watched 7 members of my immediate family die in 18 months, while I prayed ineffective prayers.

It seemed as though I grew up in a funeral home. All the while, I listened to preachers try to explain to me how it was God's will to pluck my family member as flowers for the bouquet of heaven.

Not long after that, when my own sister was facing a desperate health situation and was taking more than 30 prescribed medications a day, I decided to find out for myself what was the will of God.

I discovered that His Word was His will and His will did not make anyone sick or die. I also realized that of all of the recorded instances where people asked God if it was His will, in *every* instance He responded, "I will!" That's why one of His descriptive names is, "Jehovah Raphe," meaning "the God that healeth thee."

If it is not God's will to save you, set you free, and heal you, then why didn't He give you at least one illustration in His Word where it wasn't His will?

If it is the Lord's will to heal you, then you must settle in your heart once and for all that God did not make you sick. If He put sickness on you, He had to steal it to get it, because He does not possess sickness. He does not have cancer, disease, depression, or oppression reserved somewhere in heaven for you. Where would He keep it? Anything which comes into His presence that is contrary to His nature cannot survive.

You can settle the question of God's will to heal you right now. You don't have to be confused and wonder whether He gave you sickness or not. Therefore, if He didn't give it to you, that means you don't have any business holding onto it!

If you still question God's will concerning your healing, then meditate upon this. The Bible says, "Or what man is there of you, whom if his son ask bread, will he give him a stone? Or if he ask a fish, will he give him a serpent? If ye then, being evil, know how to give good gifts unto your children, how much more shall your Father which is in heaven give good things to them that ask him? (Matthew 7:9-11). Your heavenly Father only gives good gifts, and every good and perfect gift proceeds from Him, the Father of lights, with whom there is no variableness nor shadow of turning. (See James 1:17.)

Not long ago I had a knot appear on my side. The first thing the devil reminded me of was the 7 members of my immediate family who died in 18 months, 5 of them with cancer. The devil would try to plant thoughts in my mind that I had cancer. But I looked in God's Holy writ and found Psalm 107, "Then they cry unto the Lord in their trouble, and he saveth them out of their distresses. He sent his word, and healed them, and delivered them from their destructions" (vv. 19,20).

I began to thank my heavenly Father that I was healed even though it hurt just to touch that bump in my body. I put a bandage on it, and one night, in my sleep the bandage came off. I got up, and there was the knot laying in the bed. Today, there is no sign in my body that it ever existed! Jesus is, has always been, and will always be a healer!

The Bible states that you make "the word of God of none effect through your tradition, which ye have delivered: and many such like things do ye" (Mark 7:13). That's why when the Lord sends His Word, it doesn't heal you. You void it when you begin to question whether it is His will to heal you or not.

Can you imagine how God must feel? He sent His only Son, Jesus Christ, and allowed Him to bear our sicknesses on the tree. He was beaten and whipped until His flesh hung around his legs like ribbons, so that you and I would never have to bear sickness again. But then we question His will in the matter.

Always remember, healing is not a promise. Healing is a fact! The King of Glory didn't promise you anything. He established it by His Word. Write it down in your day planner. Put it on note cards on your refrigerator or bathroom mirror. It is vital to know what God's will is!

The end of the leper's story in the Gospel of Mark is truly happy! Jesus' answer to this desperate man's question of His will to be made whole was, "I will; be thou clean" (1:41b).

CAN JESUS HEAL YOU?

The answer to the second question, "Can Jesus heal you?" can be found in the Gospel of Mark as well:

And one of the multitude answered and said, Master, I have brought unto thee my son, which hath a dumb spirit; and wheresoever he taketh him, he teareth him: and he foameth, and gnasheth with his teeth, and pineth away: and I spake to thy disciples that they should cast him out; and they could not.

He answereth him, and saith, O faithless generation, how long shall I be with you? how long shall I suffer you? bring him unto me. And they brought him unto him: and when he saw him, straightway the spirit tare him; and he fell on the ground, and wallowed foaming.

And he asked his father, How long is it ago since this came unto him? And he said, Of a child. And ofttimes it hath cast him into the fire, and into the waters, to destroy him: but if thou canst do any thing, have compassion on us, and help us.

Jesus said unto him, If thou canst believe, all things are possible to him that believeth. And straightway the father of the child cried out, and said with tears, Lord, I believe; help thou mine unbelief.

When Jesus saw that the people came running together, he rebuked the foul spirit, saying unto him, Thou dumb and deaf spirit, I charge thee, come out of him, and enter no more into him. And the spirit cried, and rent him sore, and

came out of him: and he was as one dead; inso-
much that many said, He is dead. But Jesus
took him by the hand, and lifted him up; and he
arose (9:17-27).

The first thing I want you to notice is that all of the king's horses, and all the king's men couldn't put this child back together again. My question is: Why were they messing around with all the king's horses and all the king's men, or disciples? Why didn't they just go talk to the King of kings and the Lord of lords? That's why Jesus said, "Bring the boy to me!"

Since the disciples couldn't do anything for this father's son, he now directs his attention to Jesus and says, in essence, "Can you heal my boy?"

Jesus looked at the man and said, "It is not a question of what I can do but, rather, of what you can believe. For if you can believe, all things are possible to him that believeth!" The same is true for you! It is not a question of whether or not Jesus can heal you. The question lies instead with you. What can you believe him to do?

To illustrate this point perfectly, many years ago there was a little girl named Betty. She was born with her limbs twisted one on top of the other.

By the age of 14 she had never had a piece of clothing on her body because she was so grossly twisted and deformed. Her entire life was spent laying in a bed. She never fed herself because she only could eat through a tube. On rare occasions she could sip a little bit through a straw.

One day, she said to her little denominational mother, "Momma, Jesus . . ." Her mother stopped her and said, "I know what you're going to say because Jesus told me, too."

He had appeared to both of them and said, "At 2:00 in the afternoon on Sunday, I'm going to come in your room, and I'm going to heal you."

So Betty and her momma made a plan. Betty said, "Momma, here's what I need you to do. I can't turn over on my own, but right over there I can see the wall. Momma, please get me a dress and a pair of patent leather shoes, and hang them on that wall. Because between now and Sunday afternoon, I want to look at them."

Betty and her momma told the church they were attending what God was about to do. The pastor finished service early that Sunday afternoon so everyone could get over to Betty's home by 2:00 in the afternoon. The news media also showed up to see what they thought God was not going to do.

But at 2:00 p.m. sharp a little white cloud appeared in the living room. It moved down a hallway and went into Betty's room. It stopped right over the foot of her bed. She tried her best to touch it but she couldn't because of her twisted limbs. Finally, she fell over in exhaustion. God told her later the reason He would not allow her to touch the cloud was so she would know her healing didn't have anyhing to do with her and had everything to do with Him.

As the cloud moved over Betty's bed, eyewitnesses from the news media said it sounded like cracking limbs. It was Betty's bones which were cracking and moving back into place. After fourteen years as a hopeless invalid, she came out of that bed for the first time. Her mother helped her put on her new dress and shoes. Neither fit properly but that didn't matter.

She went running around the house and outside with those shoes flopping, because she knew that not only was it Jesus' will to heal, but He can heal, too!

WILL YOU BE MADE WHOLE?

The last question which must be answered regarding your healing is, "Will you be made whole?" The Gospel of John shows what our response should be:

> *Now there is at Jerusalem by the sheep market a pool, which is called in the Hebrew tongue Bethesda, having five porches.*
>
> *In these lay a great multitude of impotent folk, of blind, halt, withered, waiting for the moving of the water. For an angel went down at a certain season into the pool, and troubled the water: whosoever then first after the troubling of the water stepped in was made whole of whatsoever disease he had.*
>
> *And a certain man was there, which had an infirmity thirty and eight years. When Jesus saw him lie, and knew that he had been now a long time in that case, he saith unto him, Wilt thou be made whole?*
>
> *The impotent man answered him, Sir, I have no man, when the water is troubled, to put me into the pool: but while I am coming, another steppeth down before me. Jesus saith unto him, Rise, take up thy bed, and walk. And immediately the man was made whole, and took up his bed, and walked: and on the same day was the sabbath (5:2-9).*

Right now, even as you read this book, I believe Jesus is asking, "Will you be made whole?" People always try to argue with Jesus while He asks, "Do you want to be made whole?"

The man by the pool of Bethesda answered this question by saying, "I don't have any man." Why do you need a man? A man can't heal you anyway, only Jesus can!

The Lord, in His infinite mercy, said, "Rise, take up your bed and walk."

The moment Jesus said those words, that man did not have the ability to do anything He just asked him to do. But he took a step of faith, and when he did, strength entered his limbs and muscles. Not only did he get up off of his bed of affliction, he carried it away with him.

I'm reminded of a story that a great preacher and teacher of the Word of God has shared many times. He was in his hotel room preparing to speak at a meeting, when the enemy attacked his body with pneumonia. His chest tightened up to the point he could barely breathe, and he began coughing.

The Lord let him know that it wasn't his affliction, but there was someone else there in that condition. The devil was trying to stop him from preaching, because God desired to do a great miracle there that night. In fact, God said to him, "There's going to be a blind man there tonight, and I am going to open his eyes."

My friend went to the meeting, and there was a gentleman there who had a great business. Many were talking about him and what a great blessing he was to the kingdom of God.

The Lord had told my preacher friend, "When you get there all I want you to do is share the story of blind Bartimaeus, and I will open that man's eyes."

This wasn't what my friend had prepared but he said, "Lord, I will do what you want me to do."

The businessman they were talking about earlier was in church that evening and was introduced to share his testimony. This same man just happened to be blind. He gave his testimony, went back over to his seat and sat down.

As he had been directed by the Spirit of God, the preacher got up and began to share the story of blind Bartimaeus. He shared how he cried out when everybody tried to get him to be quiet, including Jesus' disciples. The more someone tried to shut him up, he cried all the more! My friend knew that businessman couldn't see, but he stood right in front of him and said, "Blind Bartimaeus cried out! He cried out to God! And when he cried out and would not be silenced, God opened his eyes! The blind man cried out!"

My friend said, "The whole service the man sat there, never moved, and never said a word." He said it was one of the most disappointing things he ever witnessed. When he returned to his hotel room, the Lord told him, "I have been trying to heal him for years, but I can't get him to do what I say."

That's why I am sharing the truths found within this book. There is a prophetic word permeating every page. In this hour of double portion, God has declared, "If you will do this, I will do that."

Will you be made whole? Will you take a step of faith?

The church is filled with people who have sold out to a victim mentality. Why? Because it's so easy and you don't have to do anything to become a victim. Not only is it easy, you gain attention. If you're the victim, then you can't help the condition you're in. Therefore, you can't take responsibility for yourself.

We need some desperation again. For too long we've sat idly by, shouted at someone else's miracle, and stayed in our sickness, disease, poverty and bondage. We need to refuse to be refused and deny to be denied!

Do you know that the reason Jesus came out of that tomb was because it was not possible for death to hold Him? That Word was waiting to resurrect the dead, cold body of the Lamb slain before the foundations of the world. So, when they put Him in the borrowed tomb, that Word said, "My time has come."

Your time has come. This is the time to believe God with everything in you. What I have shared with you is destined to change your future if you will allow it to. I believe you can move into your miracle by an act of obedience just like the man at the pool of Bethesda did.

The tangible anointing is present to give you the miracle you have been believing for. There is virtue waiting to flow into you from Jesus' riven side. It was the same for the people touched by Peter's shadow. The Book of Acts declares, "And believers were the more added to the Lord, multitudes both of men and women.) Insomuch that they brought forth the sick into the streets, and laid them on beds and couches, that at the least the shadow of Peter passing by might overshadow some of them" (Acts 5:14, 15).

Those who were touched by Paul's ministry experienced the same thing also, for Acts 19:11,12 say, "And God wrought special miracles by the hands of Paul: So that from his body were brought unto the sick handkerchiefs or aprons, and the diseases departed from them, and the evil spirits went out of them."

Before we move on to the next chapter, I want to pray for you to receive Jesus' saving, healing, and delivering power into your life as well:

Father, I set myself in agreement right now with each person who reads this book. I believe that your healing power is manifesting in their lives as your Word takes root in their spirit. Lord, I call you to record this day that you bless them in the land that you sware to give them. You take sickness and disease and remove it from the midst of them. Their children call them blessed, and they are blessed coming in and blessed going out.

I declare to you be saved, healed, delivered, and prosperous, in the name of Jesus. Amen.

Chapter Four

Our God Is Able

At this moment, if you have accepted Jesus Christ as your personal Savior, you have His power available to you —which is sufficient to deliver you in every arena of conflict. Already resident on the inside of you is the double portion of power, the authority, and the anointing to break you through to victory.

You may not feel like you have that anointing, but it is still there. It is all a matter of whether you use it or not. You may not feel able to drive sickness, pain, discouragement and depression from your midst, but you have enabling power on the inside of you.

NOW UNTO HIM WHO IS ABLE

God did not offer salvation to people from their sinful, hopeless condition to leave them as He found them. Rather, salvation only prepares you to go to heaven. The baptism of the Holy Ghost prepares you to live here on earth. Look at what the book of Ephesians says,

> *Now unto him that is able to do exceeding abundantly above all that we ask or think,*

according to the power that worketh in us. (3:20).

Did you notice that this verse begins with the word, "now"? God has already placed a "now" power on the inside of you to defeat your adversary. He did not say you have to wait until tomorrow, next week, or until you complete your Sunday school class. You have power on the inside of you right now!

The second thing this verse says is "unto Him." Your miracle is not about you. It is about the Holy One alive on the inside of you. He is the Author and Finisher of your faith. He is the "I am that I am." He is the God of heaven and earth. He is Elohim. He is Jehovah Jireh, Jehovah Rohi, and Jehovah Tsidkenu just to name a few!

The third thing to recognize in this Scripture is that it says, "Now unto Him who is able."

You may not be able, and you may be weary. But I have good news: God is able!

Let weakness lie limp on the shoulder of God. He is able. Let them throw Daniel in the lion's den. He will reckon his position and turn his face toward Jerusalem. He will offer his prayer to God, pillow his head in the shaggy mane of the lion, and sleep like a baby all night long, because he knows his God is able.

There is something more important than that God is able. He is able to do whatever you need. When you are walking through the valley of the downhearted, the Lord can lift you up on a mountain of rejoicing. Almighty God can cool the fevered brow of your infant child. The Lord of Hosts can pay the mortgage when there is no money in your bank account. The King of Glory can put bread on the table when you don't have a dollar to change. The Great Physician can drive cancer out of your body. The

King and Priest of your life can prosper your ministry, and increase you in every area of your life!

That power is working in your life right now. You may not be able to see it, but it is working. You may not have received a clean bill of health yet, but that power on the inside of you is on the job.

You may not be able to see the angels moving into position to retrieve the answer to your prayer, but rest assured they are on the move! Remember, Daniel prayed for twenty-one days for his answer, even though the angel was dispatched immediately when he formed the words upon his lips to make his petition known.

You may not see the sickness leaving your body, but you can know better than you know your name that it is dissipating. God's power and anointing are affecting a healing, deliverance, and cure.

The power resident on the inside of you can put your family back together. The anointing can apprehend your lost and dying children who have rebelled against God.

As I shared earlier, the anointing produces motion against satanic resistance in your life. God is working with you right now, confirming His Word. He is removing all doubt in your life by performing indisputable acts of authority.

But did you know that the greatest exertion of energy always comes at the point of opposition? In other words, it takes far less energy to sustain a body in motion than to get a body moving which has been at rest. For example, I've heard a jet airplane will burn ten times the fuel two to three minutes after its initial takeoff than it will burn at cruising altitude.

Ask yourself this question, "Do I have any resistance in my life?" Almost everyone has some form of resistance or another.

If there is no resistance, that power is not working. Most Christians have resistance against them, regardless of how seemingly big or small. If you have resistance, you know God's power is at work within you, because it is producing motion against every obstacle you are facing.

The devil may try to push you out and take you out. But God already has His plan in action to keep you in! Make this declaration of faith: "Miracles are working in me. Faith is at work in me. Favor is working in me. It's working, it's working, it's working in me!"

The last thing we need to learn from Ephesians 3:20 is that God is able to do exceeding abundantly above all that we ask or think according to the power at work within us!

What is that power?

There are two Greek words used for power in the New Testament. They are "dunamis," and "exousia." Dunamis means to be able or possible; a force; especially miraculous power.[1]

According to this Scripture, the word used for power is dunamis. It is a force at work within you to produce the miraculous! It is called the anointing!

Power is sometimes used with the word authority. One can have power to perform a task but not the authority to do it.

The ultimate display of the power of God is found in redemption. (See 1 Corinthians 1:18,24.) The preaching of the Gospel is followed by the power of the Holy Spirit. (See 1 Corinthians 2:4.) Miracles are indicative of power. (See Matthew 11:21,23.) At the culmination of all things, God will rule and reign in power (See Revelation 11:17.)

JESUS — A MAN OF POWER AND AUTHORITY

Jesus Christ had both power and authority. It was displayed after He descended the Mountain of Temptation, where He was tempted by Satan forty days and forty nights.

The Bible says that Jesus returned in the "dunamis" power of the Spirit, and a fame or a rumor went about through the region. (See Luke 4:14.)

Let me just interject this here. I want people to talk about me. I want the world to see so much of the presence of God on me that they begin to spread a rumor that I have been with Jesus! The Gospel of Luke continues:

> *And he taught in their synagogues, being glorified of all. And he came to Nazareth, where he had been brought up: and, as his custom was, he went into the synagogue on the sabbath day, and stood up for to read.*
>
> *And there was delivered unto him the book of the prophet Esaias. And when he had opened the book, he found the place where it was written, The Spirit of the Lord is upon me, because he hath anointed me to preach the gospel to the poor; he hath sent me to heal the brokenhearted, to preach deliverance to the captives, and recovering of sight to the blind, to set at liberty them that are bruised, to preach the acceptable year of the Lord.*
>
> *And he closed the book, and he gave it again to the minister, and sat down. And the eyes of all them that were in the synagogue were fastened on him (vv. 15-20).*

Jewish historians say that in every Jewish synagogue there was a distinctive seat. No one ever sat there because it was reserved for the coming Messiah. But Jesus sat in this seat after He read from the scroll given to Him, declaring Himself to be this promised Messiah.

The people became so incensed that Luke goes on to recount how they grabbed Him by the nape of the neck to throw Him from the brow of the hill.

In essence they said, "Who does He think He is?" I think it was very evident who He thought He was. It was evident that He had come down from the mountain full of the power of God, and He was ready to announce to the world who He was, as well!

WHOM DO MEN SAY THAT I AM?

I think it is time that we look at the world and begin to tell them who Jesus is. We have hidden behind our religion long enough! While walking upon the earth, Jesus asked His disciples,

Whom do men say that I the Son of man am?

And they said, Some say that thou art John the Baptist: some, Elias; and others, Jeremias, or one of the prophets. He saith unto them, But whom say ye that I am? And Simon Peter answered and said, Thou art the Christ, the Son of the living God.

> *And Jesus answered and said unto him,*
> *Blessed art thou, Simon Barjona: for flesh and*
> *blood hath not revealed it unto thee, but my*
> *Father which is in heaven. And I say also unto*
> *thee, That thou art Peter, and upon this rock I*
> *will build my church; and the gates of hell shall*
> *not prevail against it (Matthew 16:13b-18).*

Notice that Peter's response was, "Thou art the Christ." That word Christ means the "Anointed One."[2] Jesus is the Anointed One who destroys every yoke. He is the Son of the living God.

Let's look again at Luke 4. First, we know that Jesus is the Alpha and the Omega. He is the beginning and the end. He was with God from the beginning, for the book of Genesis says, "And God said, Let us make man in our image, after our likeness" (1:26a).

Why then, must God anoint Jesus, who is also God? The reason can be found in Philippians 2:6,7 which state that Jesus, "Who, being in the form of God, thought it not robbery to be equal with God: but made himself of no reputation, and took upon him the form of a servant, and was made in the likeness of men."

Jesus did not heal and deliver people because He was the Son of God. Acts 10:37,38 expound,

> *That word, I say, ye know, which was pub-*
> *lished throughout all Judaea, and began from*
> *Galilee, after the baptism which John preached;*
> *how God anointed Jesus of Nazareth with the*
> *Holy Ghost and with power: who went about*
> *doing good, and healing all that were oppressed*
> *of the devil; for God was with him.*

Jesus had power and authority because He was the Son of Man. He did not go around calling Himself the Son of God. Even when demons, whom Jesus cast out of many people, cried out that He was the Christ, the Son of God, He rebuked them. (See Luke 4:41.)

Our Lord and Savior, Jesus Christ, came in dunamis power to defeat the works of darkness on the earth. But He didn't stop there. Luke 10:19 proclaims, "Behold, I give unto you power to tread on serpents and scorpions, and over all the power of the enemy: and nothing shall by any means hurt you." He left us an inheritance, a double portion of power to perform greater works on His behalf.

POWER IN EARTHEN VESSELS

The Bible said in another place, "But we have this treasure in earthen vessels, that the excellency of the power may be of God, and not of us" (2 Corinthians 4:7).

There is something alive on the inside of you that is bigger than you, and it is not only bigger than you, it's bigger than all your problems. It is bigger than all your fears. It is bigger than any mountain that you can or cannot see. The Gospel of John states,

> *He that believeth on me, as the scripture hath said, out of his belly shall flow rivers of living water. (But this spake he of the Spirit, which they that believe on him should receive: for the Holy Ghost was not yet given; because that Jesus was not yet glorified.) (7:38,39).*

These verses describe how your spirit becomes the generator which takes the Word of God and changes it into the fuel that the Holy Ghost uses to produce the anointing in your life.

This anointing removes every burden and destroys every yoke. It will set the captive at liberty. It will deliver you even if you don't know you are bound. It will bless you far beyond human comprehension.

God is not limited by your mental reasoning or your natural resources! He is not confined to your philosophical understanding of Him! Jehovah is not contained in your little religious box. Rather, He wants to burst forth and show you He is bigger than we have preached, bigger than we have taught, and bigger than we have heard! And, He is living in you! You have an unction from the Holy Spirit!

It doesn't matter what you are bound by. It doesn't matter what sickness has attached itself to your body. You can break the back of your adversary through the anointing of God.

The Apostle Paul had his arms and legs chained to a wall with the sewage and sludge of a Roman city running around him; rats and infestations of every kind; and, water from the streets above him dripping upon his head; yet, he said, "But God, who is rich in mercy, for his great love wherewith he loved us, even when we were dead in sins, hath quickened us together with Christ, (by grace ye are saved;) and hath raised us up together, and made us sit together in heavenly places in Christ Jesus" (Ephesians 2:4-6).

Had Paul lost his mind? What was he thinking? Though he was bound with physical chains, he knew nothing could stop the Word of God, so he declared,

"Wherein I suffer trouble, as an evil doer, even unto bonds; but the word of God is not bound" (2 Timothy 2:9).

Allow me to paraphrase. Paul said, "It doesn't matter what kind of chain they put on me as long as I can speak God's Word! I will talk like a free man." You have an anointing, too, that no matter what the devil tries to bind you with God already possesses the key to set you free!

THE FORCE IS WITH YOU!

Jesus' life force is with you! It is an anointing which causes the world to focus its gaze upon you and say, "What is different about you?" You go through trouble and tribulation like they do, but you don't throw your hands up in despair. You have opportunities to quit and give up, but you remember that "he who endureth to the end shall be saved" (Matthew 10:22b).

Sinners do not understand the saint who can make it through life's toughest times. But we know that it is not us, but Christ in us which is the hope of glory. (See Colossians 1:27.) He has vanquished death and is alive on the inside of us. The Lord is not out there somewhere over the rainbow. He is right here, as it were, with His hand inside you. And, when you speak, it is not you speaking; it is Him speaking through you.

Jesus is the only one that ever died to bring His own will into effect, only to rise from the dead to watch over it. He wants to make sure everybody receives what He said they were supposed to have—a double portion!

You are not an ordinary person living in an ordinary world! Things don't have to go from bad to worse at your house. You don't have to die because a doctor said so. Your children don't have to get sick just because there is a "bug" going around. Why? Because you have an unction of the Holy Ghost!

This same anointing will propel you through every barrier directly into your breakthrough. Every problem that you face is nothing more than an opportunity. Every grave is just a promised resurrection. Every cross is just an opening to display God's power. Every trial is just an occasion for a testimony.

Always remember that accepting Jesus as your personal Lord and Savior prepares you to live in heaven. But receiving the infilling of the Holy Ghost equips you with power to live every day upon this earth.

The disciples were of no earthly good until they were baptized in the Holy Ghost. That is the reason Jesus said, "Go tarry ye in Jerusalem until you be endued with power from on high." (See Luke 24:49.) He could have said, "Don't leave the Upper Room without this anointing."

It is the command of God for believers to be filled with His Spirit. Ephesians 5:17,18 say, "Wherefore be ye not unwise, but understanding what the will of the Lord is. And be not drunk with wine, wherein is excess; but be filled with the Spirit."

It was very clear when New Testament believers were anointed and filled with the Holy Ghost. For the Book of Acts records, "And they were all filled with the Holy Ghost, and began to speak with other tongues, as the Spirit gave them utterance" (2:4). And Peter, filled with the Holy Ghost, preached to the multitude (See Acts 4:5-10.) "And they were all filled with the Holy Spirit and spoke the word of God with boldness"(4:31b). Stephen, "being full of the Holy Ghost, looked up stedfastly into heaven, and saw the glory of God, and Jesus standing on the right hand of God" (7:55). "And the disciples were filled with joy, and with the Holy Ghost" (13:52).

You can't be anointed by God and expect to keep it a secret. The anointing is never for you. It is always for somebody else.

That is the reason I think it's time we answered the question of a scornful world and an untoward generation who asks, "Who is the Lord, that we should serve Him? Is Buddha God, is Mohammed God, or is Jesus God?"

We need to send them word that the blind see, the deaf hear, the lame walk, the dumb speak, marriages are put back together, cancer is gone, arthritis disappears, and addictions are broken.

These things don't happen in the name of Mohammed. They do not change in the name of Buddha. But it's in the name above every name, Jesus Christ, for the Word of God declares, "Wherefore God also hath highly exalted him, and given him a name which is above every name: that at the name of Jesus every knee should bow, of things in heaven, and things in earth, and things under the earth; and that every tongue should confess that Jesus Christ is Lord, to the glory of God the Father" (Philippians 2:9-11).

It's time the world knew about the Jesus we claim to serve! He is Abel's sacrifice and Noah's rainbow. He is Abraham's well and Jacob's ladder. He is Isaiah's fig poultice and Hezekiah's sundial.

The Anointed One, Jesus Christ, is the wheel in the middle of the wheel. He is the fourth man in life's fiery furnace. He is the Lord of the lamp stand. He is the Christ of the candlestick. His eyes are like fire, his hair is like flaxen wool and His feet are like brass.

Jesus Christ has come to destroy the iron bars—which the adversary has raised against you—through His anointing. He is present with you now as Master, Savior, Redeemer, Healer, Deliverer, Sanctifier, and Provider to meet you at the point of your need. Just reach out and touch Him and receive His enabling power!

Chapter Five

A Rich Inheritance

When my pastor and mentor, Dr. Lester Sumrall, was alive, every time he would come to town, I would try to get him the finest suite in the most beautiful hotel in town. He always said, "I don't want to go there." So he would stay with me and my family.

One time I asked Dr. Sumrall, "Why do you not want to stay in the hotel when they have room service and everything you need?"

He responded, "One reason. I want to sleep in your bed."

He didn't want to sleep in my bed to get what I have. He wanted to sleep in my bed to leave what he had. He wanted to leave a rich inheritance, the tangible anointing.

I would tell my wife, Joni, to leave those sheets on the bed . . . because we were going to sleep in the anointing that night!

AN ANOINTING YOU DIDN'T PAY FOR

As part of the body of Christ you have a rich inheritance, a double portion, from great men and women of the faith who have gone before you. That anointing is available to you; all you have to do is claim it.

Before Israel entered the Promised Land and drove out their adversaries, the Lord gave them a promise through His servant, Moses. Deuteronomy 6:10-12 declare:

> *And it shall be, when the Lord thy God shall have brought thee into the land which he sware unto thy fathers, to Abraham, to Isaac, and to Jacob, to give thee great and goodly cities, which thou buildedst not, and houses full of all good things, which thou filledst not, and wells digged, which thou diggedst not, vineyards and olive trees, which thou plantedst not; when thou shalt have eaten and be full; then beware lest thou forget the Lord, which brought thee forth out of the land of Egypt, from the house of bondage.*

Olive yards mentioned in this passage of Scripture could be likened to the anointing. It is just like God told the Israelites, "There is an anointing waiting for you that you didn't even pay for. It is waiting for you."

I'm reminded of the anointing from a big two-fisted plumber, named Smith Wigglesworth, who lived in London. He was one of the greatest apostles who ever lived. He never read another publication other than the Bible. People were raised from the dead by the anointing of the Holy Ghost upon his life.

In one particular instance, he grabbed a man out of a casket, stood him against a wall and commanded him to live. There were seven documented resurrections from the dead in his ministry.

During another time in Brother Wigglesworth's life, he stayed in a home, as it was their custom in those days, in the town where he was holding a revival campaign. He stayed in the husband and wife's bedroom. The woman was saved but her husband was unsaved.

After several days of ministry, Brother Wigglesworth was called to go to another town, and he was leaving in the middle of the day. But before he could leave, the woman ran out of the house and said, "Wait, you can't go. My husband is not yet saved."

Brother Wigglesworth turned around and said, "Just don't change the sheets!

So the woman didn't change the sheets. The next night when her husband was in bed asleep, he sprang from his bed. He said, "My God, I'm lost without Jesus! Pray for me; I need to get saved!"

On a separate occasion, Brother Wigglesworth was on a trolley car in London, and a Catholic priest was seated next to him. When Brother Wigglesworth arose to walk to the back of the trolley car, he passed this Catholic priest. Immediately, the priest fell out of his chair and began to weep. He grabbed Brother Wigglesworth by the leg, and said, "My God, man, you convict me of my sin." Brother Wigglesworth never said a word. He was just going through his everyday life, with one exception. The anointing and presence of the Holy Spirit was upon him!

I have shown you throughout this book that the anointing is a tangible substance. It was in Moses' rod and Elisha's bones. It was in Peter's shadow and Paul's handkerchiefs and aprons. Not only is the anointing something which can be manifested in a person or thing, it can also be transferred.

THE TRANSFERENCE OF THE ANOINTING

That same anointing which was present on Brother Wigglesworth was transferred to Dr. Lester Sumrall, and he transferred it to me and this final generation.

People used to run up to me all the time and stick their heads out, wanting me to pray for them to receive an anointing. One particular instance comes to mind . . . a lady who was attending one of my meetings grabbed my hand and stuck it on her forehead. She said, "What are you getting?"

I responded, "A sweaty palm. I am not getting anything."

Many go around seeking a double portion from a man or woman of God. But the anointing upon their lives, including mine, came at a price.

My parents both worked two jobs. For a time, we lived in an apartment over a bar, with one bedroom for four people. When I was growing up, my mother had to cut out cardboard and put it in the bottom of her shoes to walk in the snow to her second job. And, as I mentioned earlier, before I understood about God's healing nature, seven members of my immediate family died within eighteen months.

Most people do not want to pay this kind of price for the anointing. In reality, everyone has trials and circumstances they go through to walk in the anointing upon their lives. No one really knows what it costs to be you.

When I first entered the ministry, I knew a man whom—every time I came in contact with him—I just sensed God on him. Did you ever get around somebody where you could just sense God on them? I thought maybe this anointing would come upon me after being in the ministry several years.

So I inquired of a mutual friend and said how much I would love to walk in that same anointing someday, where you just sense the presence of God.

This friend countered, "Well, you can. Somebody told me I could."

I found out the anointing doesn't come with years of ministry experience. Years have nothing to do with it. It comes from laying aside every weight which does so easily beset you, seeking the face of God, and paying the price for it.

But as I shared at the beginning of this chapter, the book of Deuteronomy declares that the Lord will give you olive yards, or the anointing, that you didn't pay for. (See 6:11.) The King of Glory wants to give you anointings you never had to pay for. Why? Because we are living in the final hours of human history, and He has to do a quick work!

Time is accelerating. God doesn't have the time to take you through everything past generations faced to get where they were in Him.

I don't care what religion has told you. Every believer can walk in the anointing. In fact, you can wear the anointing like a garment. (See Psalm 133:2.) You can have the tangible presence of God not only in your life, but also upon your body.

Some ask me why I am so blessed. It is because every time I pour myself out in ministry, whether it is through the Breakthrough broadcast, during a church service, or to meet the needs of people in any way—because of the anointing upon my life, I know that I am promised to receive back a double portion. If you will read and heed this word, I believe you will never have to pay the price for this same anointing. Rather, your heavenly Father will transfer it to you.

We should never take the tangible presence of the Lord for granted. Why? Because it is not everywhere. It is present where people are obedient to do the works that Jesus did. (See Mark 16:15-20.)

I want to see the church begin to walk in the manifested presence of God. I want to see the church display His glory.

I have had enough of dead religion. I no longer want to hear the discourses of men. I am weary of being told that God is out of reach, somewhere off in the blue by and by.

I want a God whom I can feel. I don't mean to rock your theological boat, but I want a God who comes upon me, and gets all over me.

It reminds me of the story of two men who were hunting for swamp cats. One of them caught one and began to scream. His buddy came over to him and said, "Do you want me to help you hold him?" He said, "No, I want you to help me let him go!"

I want God to get all over me to the point I don't have to ask Him where He is. I want to have the evidence of His presence in my life. I don't think there is anything wrong with looking for evidence.

John the Baptist was shut up in prison for preaching the Gospel and baptizing people. While he was there, he sent word to Jesus:

> *And said unto him, Art thou he that should come, or do we look for another? Jesus answered and said unto them, Go and shew John again those things which ye do hear and*

*see: The blind receive their sight, and the lame
walk, the lepers are cleansed, and the deaf hear,
the dead are raised up, and the poor have the
gospel preached to them (Matthew 11:3-5).*

Thank God for the tangible anointing which produces miracles. When you get involved with a prophet,
you receive a prophet's reward. (See Matthew 10:41.)
What does that mean? You unlock the prophetic gift to
your life.

A PROPHET'S REWARD

The Shunammite woman knew how to obtain a
prophet's reward. She made a chamber for Elisha so
every time he was in town he could stay with her and her
husband. One day, however, Elisha posed a question to
her:

"And he said unto him, Say now unto her, Behold,
thou hast been careful for us with all this care; what is to
be done for thee? wouldest thou be spoken for to the king,
or to the captain of the host? And she answered, I dwell
among mine own people.

"And he said, What then is to be done for her? And
Gehazi answered, Verily she hath no child, and her husband is old. And he said, Call her. And when he had
called her, she stood in the door.

"And he said, About this season, according to the
time of life, thou shalt embrace a son. And she said, Nay,
my lord, thou man of God, do not lie unto thine handmaid.
And the woman conceived, and bare a son at that season

that Elisha had said unto her, according to the time of life"
(2 Kings 4:13-17).

This woman was faithful to provide for the man of
God, and then He was faithful to bless her in return. But
her miracle died, for the Bible goes on to say:

"And when the child was grown, it fell on a day, that
he went out to his father to the reapers. And he said unto
his father, My head, my head. And he said to a lad, Carry
him to his mother.

"And when he had taken him, and brought him to his
mother, he sat on her knees till noon, and then died. And
she went up, and laid him on the bed of the man of God,
and shut the door upon him, and went out" (vv. 18-21).

This woman had every opportunity to allow the death
of her son to cause a root of bitterness in her life. Before
she conceived her son, she already told Elisha not to lie to
her. Why, then, would God give her a child who would
soon die? I believe the Lord knew that she was more than
a conqueror.

She lost her son. She lost that blessing that came to
her by a miracle. Maybe you have experienced similar
circumstances. You received your victory, but now it is
gone.

Just remember, this is just a chapter; it is not your life
story. There is more to your life. Read on a few chapters.
This Shunammite woman had already begun to formulate
a plan to recover her miracle child.

"And she called unto her husband, and said, Send me,
I pray thee, one of the young men, and one of the asses,
that I may run to the man of God, and come again. And
he said, Wherefore wilt thou go to him to day? it is neither
new moon, nor sabbath. And she said, It shall be well.
Then she saddled an ass, and said to her servant, Drive,

and go forward; slack not thy riding for me, except I bid thee.

"So she went and came unto the man of God to mount Carmel. And it came to pass, when the man of God saw her afar off, that he said to Gehazi his servant, Behold, yonder is that Shunammite: Run now, I pray thee, to meet her, and say unto her, Is it well with thee? is it well with thy husband? is it well with the child? And she answered, It is well.

"And when she came to the man of God to the hill, she caught him by the feet: but Gehazi came near to thrust her away. And the man of God said, Let her alone; for her soul is vexed within her: and the Lord hath hid it from me, and hath not told me.

"Then she said, Did I desire a son of my lord? did I not say, Do not deceive me?

"Then he said to Gehazi, Gird up thy loins, and take my staff in thine hand, and go thy way: if thou meet any man, salute him not; and if any salute thee, answer him not again: and lay my staff upon the face of the child.

"And the mother of the child said, As the Lord liveth, and as thy soul liveth, I will not leave thee. And he arose, and followed her. And Gehazi passed on before them, and laid the staff upon the face of the child; but there was neither voice, nor hearing. Wherefore he went again to meet him, and told him, saying, The child is not awaked.

"And when Elisha was come into the house, behold, the child was dead, and laid upon his bed. He went in therefore, and shut the door upon them twain, and prayed unto the Lord.

"And he went up, and lay upon the child, and put his mouth upon his mouth, and his eyes upon his eyes, and his hands upon his hands: and he stretched himself upon the child; and the flesh of the child waxed warm. Then he returned, and walked in the house to and fro; and went up, and stretched himself upon him: and the child sneezed seven times, and the child opened his eyes.

"And he called Gehazi, and said, Call this Shunammite. So he called her. And when she was come in unto him, he said, Take up thy son.

"Then she went in, and fell at his feet, and bowed herself to the ground, and took up her son, and went out" (vv. 22-37).

This Shunammite woman left her dead son in the prophet's room and traveled, we don't know how far, to where the man of God dwelt. Upon seeing her, the prophet, Elisha, asked, "Is it well?" She announced, "It is well."

She was speaking prophetically. She learned from Elisha that her words meant something. He said she would conceive a son and she did. Because of this she found out that her words have power. The power of life and death is in the tongue! (See Proverb 18:21.)

Notice that this woman was not some New Testament saint who was infused and inundated with the Word of the living God. But she understood His anointing. She realized that what had been taken from her had been given as a miracle in the first place. Therefore, if she was ever going to get it back, it was going to take a miracle. There wasn't any use for doubt and unbelief to try getting in her way. The result was Elisha prayed for the young boy, and the woman received her miracle child again!

Today, you and I have hope in the resurrected Lamb of God. He is not only with us but in us, anointing us with miracle-working power.

THE HOPE OF GLORY

If you are born again, Jesus Christ is alive on the inside of you now. This is the mystery—Christ in you. Colossians 1:27 proclaims, "To whom God would make known what is the riches of the glory of this mystery among the Gentiles; which is Christ in you, the hope of glory:"

We need to realize that the hope of the manifested tangible presence of God is in us. We need to get filled to overflowing with the Holy Spirit

That's the reason Jacob wrestled with the angel of the Lord all night long. There was too much of Jacob and not enough of God. (See Genesis 32:24-29.) Also, like John the Baptist, we must decrease so that Jesus may increase. (See John 3:30.) This should be the heartfelt prayer of every born-again, Spirit-filled, fire-baptized believer—less of us and more of Him.

Then we will shake the kingdom of darkness to its very foundation. It will be the result of the glory of God displayed on the earth through His vessels.

When you get full of the Holy Ghost, there is no room for discouragement. If you are discouraged, then you need a fresh dose of God's Spirit.

I want a deluge and downpour of the Lord's power and anointing. I want so much of the hand of God upon me, as it were, that I have to pray for Him to lift it lest I die. Why? Because you never know when God is going to call you into a situation where you need to make a withdrawal on the anointing upon your life.

Wherever we go, flames of revival will burst forth because of the anointing of God which is upon us. And, we shall remove burdens and destroy the yokes of bondage!

We are the final generation! We need to start believing, talking, and acting like it! We need to bombard the throne of God in fervent prayer and say, "God, we want our inheritance. You promised to give us the heathen for our inheritance!" We will go forth with anointing and power. And, wherever we go, men will be compelled to come to Christ because of the power of God on our lives.

A DAY OF IMPARTATION

We are destined to be a generation of Smith Wigglesworths. In his last meeting with Dr. Sumrall in London, England, just before the war, Brother Wigglesworth wrapped his arms around a young Lester Sumrall. He held him to his bosom and wept until his tears had wet Dr. Sumrall's head. And he said, "God, let the spirit of faith that is in me come into this young man."

Brother Wigglesworth looked into Dr. Sumrall's eyes and said, "I see a revival coming like the world has never known. I see thousands upon thousands running into churches, falling over altars, and crying out for God to save them.

"I see entire hospitals, and all the patients are walking out, healed from the top of their heads to the soles of their feet."

He continued, "Lester, I will never see this revival, but you will."

That revival has already begun. For those who earnestly desire and seek it, they will be part of it. I believe they will walk into hospitals, and rooms will be emptied because of the anointing of God to heal the sick.

Some may say, "That will never happen." Then the Bible is a lie. Because the Bible declares the glory of the Lord will cover the earth as the waters cover the seas! (See Habakkuk 2:14.)

There will be no place that remnant believers can go to get away from the anointing of God. It will cover the earth. We will wear the presence, the anointing, and the glory of God like a garment. Everywhere we go the sick will be healed, the lost will be saved, and men will come to God. The greatest harvest the world has ever known is coming.

Oh, what a day of impartation! That day of impartation is upon you now to receive the anointing of God!

Chapter Six

Double for Your Trouble

In the year 2001, the body of Christ actually stepped into the third day of spiritual prophetic dominion, because that was actually the beginning of the third millennium. That year many faced situations and circumstances they had never faced before. It was like when the Israelites crossed the Jordan River. God told them "Ye have not passed this way heretofore" (Joshua 3:4b).

2001 was a year of pressure. It was a time of darkness that was especially evident in the attack on America. All of the pressure and darkness was as a result of the church coming down through the birth canal of Father God and Mother Time.

A child is born of water. The children of Israel had to pass through the waters of Jordan. Remnant believers passed through the birth canal of Mother Time, as God Almighty, the Ancient of Days, gave birth to the child of His old age. This group of saints were born, like Abraham's Isaac and Jesse's David, to become a deliverer of a people born in bondage.

You were birthed for a purpose. You were birthed for a reason. God took you through what He had to take you through—in order for you to show up where He said you would be. He has been working a master plan in your life.

The Lord told Joshua, "Now hold on, for in three days you are going to pass over this Jordan, you and all the people." (See Joshua 1:11.)

But God declared in the year 2002 that it was to be the year of your greatest conquest. There is also a prophetic word about this year that you may not like.

DOUBLE FOR YOUR TROUBLE

In the year 2002, God wants to give you the same blessing He gave Job—double for your trouble. The book of Job records, "And the Lord restored Job's losses when he prayed for his friends. Indeed the Lord gave Job twice as much as he had before" (42:10 NKJV).

God doubled Job's blessing. So what if you have to walk through a valley to get over a mountain. When you receive the answer to your miracle, you will forget about what it took to get you there.

Do you remember when Jesus was with His disciples and looked across the table at Simon and said:

> *And the Lord said, Simon, Simon, behold, Satan hath desired to have you, that he may sift you as wheat (Luke 22:31).*

You could say that Satan has requisitioned you. Webster's defines requisition to mean "a formal written request for something needed."[1] Most businesses require that a requisition form be completed before a purchase is made. In other words, when you make a request, that request must be granted before you can receive whatever it is you are requesting.

So the Bible bears out that Satan not only desired, or requisitioned, to have Peter but Jesus would not give him permission! (See v. 32.)

This is similar to what happened to Job. Satan presented himself before God and requisitioned Job:

Now there was a day when the sons of God came to present themselves before the Lord, and Satan came also among them.

And the Lord said unto Satan, Whence comest thou? Then Satan answered the Lord, and said, From going to and fro in the earth, and from walking up and down in it.

And the Lord said unto Satan, Hast thou considered my servant Job, that there is none like him in the earth, a perfect and an upright man, one that feareth God, and escheweth evil?

Then Satan answered the Lord, and said, Doth Job fear God for nought? Hast not thou made an hedge about him, and about his house, and about all that he hath on every side? thou hast blessed the work of his hands, and his substance is increased in the land. But put forth thine hand now, and touch all that he hath, and he will curse thee to thy face.

And the Lord said unto Satan, Behold, all that he hath is in thy power; only upon himself put not forth thine hand. So Satan went forth from the presence of the Lord (Job 1:6-12).

Satan told the Lord that He had set a protective covering around Job, but if He would take away the covering Job would curse Him. But God knew Job better than the devil, and He knows you better than the devil does. So the devil comes and presents himself before God, and says, "Let me have that believer."

God's response is, "Go ahead. Take them if you can stand them. Hit them with your most deadly attack. They will still stand up with happy hearts and hands uplifted, and glorify me. Because they don't glorify me for what I do for them. They glorify me because I am that I am!"

This is the kind of person the Lord sees in you. You believe for your miracle, but if you don't receive it, you will praise Him anyway. You will shout and dance anyway. You will shout at the wall, and if it doesn't fall down today, you will be back tomorrow shouting again. Why? Because you have a word that victory is assured!

If you look again where Satan requisitioned to receive Peter to sift him as wheat, look at the words of encouragement Jesus gave His disciple: "But I have prayed for thee, that thy faith fail not: and when thou art converted, strengthen thy brethren" (Luke 22:32).

Jesus prayed that Peter's faith would not fail. It took faith to shout down Jericho's walls and it took faith for Peter to become a great apostle and martyr.

Jesus said, "These things I have spoken unto you, that in me ye might have peace. In the world ye shall have tribulation: but be of good cheer; I have overcome the world" (John 16:33). How do you and I overcome the world? First John 5:4 states, "For whatsoever is born of God overcometh the world: and this is the victory that overcometh the world, even our faith."

What kind of faith is it? It is that faith Jesus is praying will not fail. Don't you remember when He walked up to the tomb of Lazarus where doubt was present on the left hand and unbelief on the right? He walked up to his tomb, and the people gathered there said, "Lazarus, by this time, even smells."

Jesus could see that Lazarus was dead, and he had on the grave clothes to prove it! He could even hear the mourners as they wept over the man.

Mary and Martha came out to meet Jesus and said, "If only you would have been here, our brother would not have died. But four days ago we wrapped him in grave clothes, and we put him in the grave." (See John 11:17-32.)

But, thanks be to God, the just do not live by what they see. The just do not live by what they hear. The just do not live by what they feel. "The just live by faith" (Romans 1:17).

Jesus was fully persuaded that Lazarus was going to come out of that tomb. No one could talk Him out of it. He had hold of absolute truth. He knew that God heard Him always. (See John 11.)

Oh, if the church will ever get the revelation that they never prayed a prayer that Jesus did not hear and answer the moment they prayed it!

The Bible says, "And this is the confidence that we have in him, that, if we ask any thing according to his will, he heareth us: And if we know that he hear us, whatsoever we ask, we know that we have the petitions that we desired of him" (1 John 5:14,15).

In other words, if we know that Jesus hears us, then we have steadfast confidence and assurance that we have granted to us for our present possession those things what-soever we have requisitioned Him for. What does this mean? You have never prayed the prayer that your heavenly Father did not hear and answer the moment you prayed it.

You see, you have the emphasis on the wrong syllable in this passage of Scripture. The comma is in the wrong place, because you say it this way, "This is the confidence that we have in Him, that if we ask anything according to His will, He hears us." Rather, you should say, "If we ask anything, according to His will He hears us."

That means in eternity past, God set His will in motion to hear you! Again, though Satan has a plan to take you out, the Lord has a plan to keep you in! Romans 8:31 says it this way, "What shall we then say to these things? If God be for us, who can be against us?"

So when you are in the battle, and you are marching around the walled city of your life, and it seems like nothing is moving, don't hang your head. Lift up a shout. Don't let your shoulders be rounded. Straighten your back like a t-rail.

Why? Jericho's walls didn't come down because they shouted. The walls came down because they obeyed.

When you are in a desperate trial and tribulation remember, "Who is he that condemneth? It is Christ that died, yea rather, that is risen again, who is even at the right hand of God, who also maketh intercession for us" (Romans 8:34).

Jesus does not pray how most Christians pray. He does not pray in vague generalities, but He prays specifics. He calls your name and intercedes specifically for you, that your faith will not fail.

I have a question for you. How can your faith fail when the Lord of glory is praying for you?

THE ANOINTING IS OVERFLOWING

God has already made provision for your needs and your wants—through His anointing. The Psalmist said, "The Lord is my shepherd; I shall not want. He maketh me to lie down in green pastures: he leadeth me beside the still waters. He restoreth my soul: he leadeth me in the paths of righteousness for his name's sake.

"Yea, though I walk through the valley of the shadow of death, I will fear no evil: for thou art with me; thy rod and thy staff they comfort me" (23:1-4).

You have to see the land that God led us into is not like the land that He led us out of. The land that He led us out of was a land where you could carve your foot in the dirt, and water would flow freely from the Nile river. But the land He is leading us into is a land of hills and valleys, which drinks water of the rain of heaven.

It is not a place of self-sufficiency. This double portion anointing must come from a heavenly source. It cannot originate in the mind of a man. It cannot begin with the intellect of a denomination. The double portion must come from God.

The anointing that we are looking for is not pomp and circumstance. It is not rite, ritual, and religiosity. This anointing is not found in the cadenced creeds of creation nor in the doctrines of humanity. It is not housed in a human vessel. The anointing we seek comes from Jesus, the Anointed One.

The last two verses of this Psalm say, "Thou preparest a table before me in the presence of mine enemies:

thou anointest my head with oil; my cup runneth over. Surely goodness and mercy shall follow me all the days of my life: and I will dwell in the house of the Lord for ever" (vv. 5,6).

We need to learn to walk in the anointing. We need to have God show us how to stand up under it. And, before long, after we have learned to walk in that one, He will give us another one.

After we learn to walk in that anointing, He will wrap us in robes of righteousness, and crown us with crowns of glory. It will be so tangible that when we walk down the street, we won't have to lay hands on anyone. Rather, the mere shadows of our presence will make the lame get up.

When these Scriptures talk about how the Lord anoints our heads with oil, it can be likened to the good shepherd. Each morning, before he allowed the sheep to leave his protective fencing to graze among the rocks and stones, he poured oil over their heads.

The shepherd did this because he knew, at some point during the day, his sheep would rub their heads against sharp stones and be cut. Pouring oil over their heads in the morning prepared them for whatever would come against them that day. The balm of Gilead would already be present upon them.

What happens when the burden-removing, yoke-destroying anointing comes upon our lives? What occurs when Jesus anoints our heads with oil?

Jesus doesn't just give us a little dab or enough to get us by. Instead, He fills our cups to overflowing! It's time to throw your cup away, because God is about to pour His spirit out on you!

YOUR VICTORY IS WAITING FOR YOU

I believe God's word for 2002 is, "Cheer up; it's going to get worse!" If the devil was ever going to stop you, he should have planned to stop you in 2002. But when the devil's got a plan to take you out, God's got a shout to bring you out!

The year 2002 has prophetic significance in that it represents the law of double annunciation—when God wants to emphasize a point, He will say it twice. When He wants a city, He sits out on the Mount of Olives, looks down through the Kidron Valley and up through the Eastern Gate and on to Temple Mount and declares, "Jerusalem, Jerusalem."

When the Lord wants a miracle worker, He's not satisfied to just say, "Simon." He must say "Simon, Simon." When He needs an apostle to write two-thirds of the New Covenant, He finds him on the road to Damascus, riding his beast. He does not simply shine a light out of heaven and say, "Saul." He cries out, "Saul, Saul!"

When David wants to exclaim Jehovah's greatness and gain His attention, he does not just say, "My Lord." Instead, he declares in the law of double annunciation, "My Lord and my God."

The two "2's" in 2002 prophetically symbolize God's way of emphasizing the double. There is another law in operation here. It is the conditional response of God. It simply means if you will double this, God will double that.

If you want double power, then double your shout. If you want double in your finances, then double your giving. If you want double the breakthroughs in your prayer life, then double your prayer life. If you want double anointing, then begin to increase your ability to meet the needs of others.

God spoke to me prophetically that in this year the double, double stands for "He will do it again." Whatever your greatest victory has ever been, God is about to do it again. Do you remember when first up out of your belly there began to roll that heavenly, Holy Ghost language? Do you remember when you were first baptized in the Holy Ghost? God is about to do it again.

You may be facing the greatest struggle of your life, like the Israelites when they faced Jericho, but your victory is waiting for you just on the other side of those walls!

As I shared in chapter 2, Jericho was the second smallest of all the cities they were ever to face, yet it was the most fortified city that Joshua would face in 31 campaigns. The next battle was Ai, and after that smaller and smaller cities.

God is saying to you essentially what He said to Israel, "Hold on!" You are going to face your greatest giant. Already it may seem as if you have never experienced an attack of the adversary like you are experiencing at this very moment.

Can I tell you something? In the year 2002, you will fight the greatest fight of your life, but the victory is yours—and it's downhill from here! It doesn't matter what you face or how fortified the walls are against you. It doesn't matter how long you have been fighting to secure your victory. God has already given you the city!

You may not know how you are going to get through your situation, but all you really need to know is that you will indeed get through it. You just need to shout because you are on your way out. You are headed for more than enough, too much, overflow, and double for your trouble.

When Job made the decision to pray for his friends—the ones who had all of his so-called sins figured out and a wife that told him to curse God and die—God turned His captivity and gave him double for his trouble. He gave Job more than enough, too much, overflow, and double for his trouble!

Epilogue

Receiving Your Double Portion

As the church of the firstborn you are destined to receive not merely any blessing but a double portion blessing. The prophet, Isaiah, said it this way:

> *Instead of your shame you shall have a double portion, instead of dishonor you shall rejoice in your lot; therefore in your land you shall possess a double portion; yours shall be everlasting joy (61:7 RSV).*

Your victory will surpass what you ever dreamed and will be double of what you formerly possessed. You have God's Word on it.

Therefore, I want to add my faith to yours and believe with you that the words in this book will take root within your spirit. As we agree together, I believe you will reap the greatest miracle you have been believing for—you will receive your double portion.

"Father, I thank you that in this hour of double, double that you will increase this person's revelation and anointing. I believe you to double their freedom and the resurrection power of Christ in their lives.

"In the name of Jesus, I release to you that which I have received, an impartation of the spirit of faith to know in your weakest moment Jesus is praying for you. Even now He is calling your name, refusing to allow your faith to fail. Your greatest battle means your greatest victory.

"May you know and experience the double portion of God's peace, presence and miracle-working power in your life even now. I believe it to be so, in the mighty name of Jesus, Amen."

I believe faith is being issued to you like a river—faith for your healing, faith for your deliverance, faith for your future, faith for your family. I speak more than enough, too much, overflow, and double for all of your trouble into your life right now!

You may have wondered if your miracle would ever resurrect. But remember, if God healed and delivered you or your family before, He will do it again! Your double portion is on the way!

Double Portion Scriptures

And it shall be, when the Lord thy God shall have brought thee into the land which he sware unto thy fathers, to Abraham, to Isaac, and to Jacob, to give thee great and goodly cities, which thou buildedst not, and houses full of all good things, which thou filledst not, and wells digged, which thou diggedst not, vineyards and olive trees, which thou plantedst not; when thou shalt have eaten and be full; then beware lest thou forget the Lord, which brought thee forth out of the land of Egypt, from the house of bondage (Deuteronomy 6:10-12).

But he shall acknowledge the son of the hated for the firstborn, by giving him a double portion of all that he hath: for he is the beginning of his strength; the right of the firstborn is his (Deuteronomy 21:17).

And it came to pass, when they were gone over, that Elijah said unto Elisha, Ask what I shall do for thee, before I be taken away from thee. And Elisha said, I pray thee, let a double portion of thy spirit be upon me (2 Kings 2:9).

And Elisha died, and they buried him. And the bands of the Moabites invaded the land at the coming in of the year. And it came to pass, as they were burying a man, that, behold, they spied a band of men; and they cast the man into the sepulchre of Elisha: and when the man was let down, and touched the bones of Elisha, he revived, and stood up on his feet (2 Kings 13:20,21).

And the Lord restored Job's losses when he prayed for his friends. Indeed the Lord gave Job twice as much as he had before (Job 42:10 NKJV).

He sent his word, and healed them, and delivered them from their destructions (Psalm 107:20).

Behold, I and the children whom the Lord hath given me are for signs and for wonders in Israel from the Lord of hosts, which dwelleth in mount Zion (Isaiah 8:18).

And it shall come to pass in that day, that his burden shall be taken away from off thy shoulder, and his yoke from off thy neck, and the yoke shall be destroyed because of the anointing (Isaiah 10:27).

Instead of your shame you shall have a double portion, instead of dishonor you shall rejoice in your lot; therefore in your land you shall possess a double portion; yours shall be everlasting joy (Isaiah 61:7 RSV).

Be glad then, ye children of Zion, and rejoice in the Lord your God: for he hath given you the former rain moderately, and he will cause to come down for you the rain, the former rain, and the latter rain in the first month. And the floors shall be full of wheat, and the fats shall overflow with wine and oil (Joel 2:23,24).

For the earth shall be filled with the knowledge of the glory of the Lord, as the waters cover the sea (Habakkuk 2:14).

Or what man is there of you, whom if his son ask bread, will he give him a stone? Or if he ask a fish, will he give him a serpent? If ye then, being evil, know how to give good gifts unto your children, how much more shall your Father which is in heaven give good things to them that ask him? (Matthew 7:9-11)

He that receiveth a prophet in the name of a prophet shall receive a prophet's reward; and he that receiveth a righteous man in the name of a righteous man shall receive a righteous man's reward (Matthew 10:41).

And said unto him, Art thou he that should come, or do we look for another? Jesus answered and said unto them, Go and shew John again those things which ye do hear and see: the blind receive their sight, and the lame walk, the lepers are cleansed, and the deaf hear, the dead are raised up, and the poor have the gospel preached to them *(Matthew 11:3-5).*

And he could there do no mighty work, save that he laid his hands upon a few sick folk, and healed them. And he marvelled because of their unbelief. And he went round about the villages, teaching *(Mark 6:5,6).*

Jesus said unto him, If thou canst believe, all things are possible to him that believeth *(Mark 9:23).*

And he said unto them, Go ye into all the world, and preach the gospel to every creature. He that believeth and is baptized shall be saved; but he that believeth not shall be damned.

And these signs shall follow them that believe; In my name shall they cast out devils; they shall speak with new tongues; they shall take up serpents; and if they drink any deadly thing, it shall not hurt them; they shall lay hands on the sick, and they shall recover.

So then after the Lord had spoken unto them, he was received up into heaven, and sat on the right hand of God. And they went forth, and preached every where, the Lord working with them, and confirming the word with signs following. Amen *(Mark 16:15-20).*

The Spirit of the Lord is upon me, because he hath anointed me to preach the gospel to the poor; he hath sent me to heal the brokenhearted, to preach deliverance to the captives, and recovering of sight to the blind, to set at liberty them that are bruised, to preach the acceptable year of the Lord (Luke 4:18,19).

And the Lord said, Simon, Simon, behold, Satan hath desired to have you, that he may sift you as wheat: but I have prayed for thee, that thy faith fail not: and when thou art converted, strengthen thy brethren (Luke 22:31,32).

He that believeth on me, as the scripture hath said, out of his belly shall flow rivers of living water. (But this spake he of the Spirit, which they that believe on him should receive: for the Holy Ghost was not yet given; because that Jesus was not yet glorified) (John 7:38,39).

Verily, verily, I say unto you, He that believeth on me, the works that I do shall he do also; and greater works than these shall he do; because I go unto my Father (John 14:12.)

These things I have spoken unto you, that in me ye might have peace. In the world ye shall have tribulation: but be of good cheer; I have overcome the world (John 16:33).

But ye shall receive power, after that the Holy Ghost is come upon you: and ye shall be witnesses unto me both in Jerusalem, and in all Judaea, and in Samaria, and unto the uttermost part of the earth (Acts 1:8).

And they were all filled with the Holy Ghost, and began to speak with other tongues, as the Spirit gave them utterance (Acts 2:4).

And believers were the more added to the Lord, multitudes both of men and women.) Insomuch that they brought forth the sick into the streets, and laid them on beds and couches, that at the least the shadow of Peter passing by might overshadow some of them (Acts 5:14,15).

That word, I say, ye know, which was pub-lished throughout all Judaea, and began from Galilee, after the baptism which John preached; how God anointed Jesus of Nazareth with the Holy Ghost and with power: who went about doing good, and healing all that were oppressed of the devil; for God was with him (Acts 10:37,38).

And God wrought special miracles by the hands of Paul: So that from his body were brought unto the sick handkerchiefs or aprons, and the diseases departed from them, and the evil spirits went out of them (Acts 19:11,12).

For therein is the righteousness of God revealed from faith to faith: as it is written, The just shall live by faith (Romans 1:17).

So then faith cometh by hearing, and hearing by the word of God (Romans 10:17).

For I say, through the grace given unto me, to every man that is among you, not to think of himself more highly than he ought to think; but to think soberly, according as God hath dealt to every man the measure of faith (Romans 12:3).

But we have this treasure in earthen vessels, that the excellency of the power may be of God, and not of us (2 Corinthians 4:7).

Now unto him that is able to do exceeding abundantly above all that we ask or think, according to the power that worketh in us (Ephesians 3:20).

To whom God would make known what is the riches of the glory of this mystery among the Gentiles; which is Christ in you, the hope of glory (Colossians 1:27).

When I call to remembrance the unfeigned faith that is in thee, which dwelt first in thy grandmother Lois, and thy mother Eunice; and I am persuaded that in thee also. Wherefore I put thee in remembrance that thou stir up the gift of God, which is in thee by the putting on of my hands (2 Timothy 1:5,6).

Now faith is the substance of things hoped for, the evidence of things not seen (Hebrews 11:1).

But without faith it is impossible to please him: for he that cometh to God must believe that he is, and that he is a rewarder of them that diligently seek him (Hebrews 11:6).

By faith the walls of Jericho fell down, after they were compassed about seven days (Hebrews 11:30).

But ye are come unto mount Sion, and unto the city of the living God, the heavenly Jerusalem, and to an innumerable company of angels, to the general assembly and church of the firstborn, which are written in heaven, and to God the Judge of all, and to the spirits of just men made perfect (Hebrews 12:22,23).

By him therefore let us offer the sacrifice of praise to God continually, that is, the fruit of our lips giving thanks to his name (Hebrews 13:15).

For as the body without the spirit is dead, so faith without works is dead also (James 2:26).

But ye have an unction from the Holy One, and ye know all things (1 John 2:20).

Ye are of God, little children, and have overcome them: because greater is he that is in you, than he that is in the world (1 John 4:4).

For whatsoever is born of God overcometh the world: and this is the victory that over-cometh the world, even our faith (1 John 5:4).

And this is the confidence that we have in him, that, if we ask any thing according to his will, he heareth us: and if we know that he hear us, whatsoever we ask, we know that we have the petitions that we desired of him (1 John 5:14,15).

Notes

Chapter 1

1. *Webster's New Collegiate Dictionary*, G. & C. Merriam Cr., Springfield, MA, 1977.

Chapter 4

1. *Biblesoft's New Exhaustive Strong's Numbers and Concordance with Expanded Greek-Hebrew Dictionary*, Biblesoft and International Bible Translators, Inc., 1994.

2. Ibid.

Chapter 6

1. Noah Webster, *Webster's II New Riverside University Dictionary*, (Howard Webber, Boston: Houghton Mifflin company, 1984), page 936.

About the Author

Rod Parsley is pastor of World Harvest Church in Columbus, Ohio, a dynamic megachurch with more than 12,000 in attendance weekly, that touches lives worldwide. He is also a highly sought-after crusade and conference speaker who delivers a life-changing message to raise the standards of physical purity, moral integrity, and spiritual intensity.

Parsley also hosts *Breakthrough*, a daily and weekly television broadast, seen by millions across America and around the world. He also oversees Bridge of Hope Missions and Outreach, World Harvest Bible College, and Harvest Preparatory School. He and his wife, Joni, have two children, Ashton and Austin.

For more information about Breakthrough, World Harvest Church or to receive a product list of the many books, audio and video tapes by Rod Parsley, write or call:

Breakthrough
P.O. Box 32932
Columbus, Ohio 43232-0932
(614) 837-1990 (Office)

For information about World Harvest Bible College, write or call:

World Harvest Bible College
P.O. Box 32901
Columbus, Ohio 43232-0901
(614) 837-4088

If you need prayer, Breakthrough Prayer Warriors are ready to pray with you
24 hours a day, 7 days a week at:
(614) 837-3232

Visit Rod Parsley at his website address:
<u>www.breakthrough.net</u>